"The authors of this book develop the concept of human connectivity to bring us to a new level of understanding of how and why it is so important. Development of clusters of new technology companies, science parks and innovation centres, has demonstrated conclusively the importance of human connectivity for the development and success of technological innovation and transfer; it is sometimes more important than the technology itself"
– Alan Barrell, Professor of Entrepreneurship, Cambridge Learning Gateway

"All aspects of life involve relationships and that includes the business world. Sadly, this is often forgotten not only by those involved in business but also by those criticising businesses or seeking to reform business laws and practices. The result is an impasse. This book offers us a possible way forward, not merely by suggesting solutions to particular issues, but by inviting us to look at the problem in a different way. It deserves to be widely read and considered"
– Richard Godden, Partner, Linklaters LLP, U.K.

"The world is not what it used to be. One of the many reasons for this is the change of thinking in the corporate world that the shareholder had primacy of place amongst other stakeholders. In our resource constrained and climate changing world, corporate capitalism has changed from being exclusively in favour of the shareholder to inclusive, with the board taking account of the needs interests and expectations and concerns of stakeholders pertinent to the business. The board in discharging its duty of care to the company should always make a decision in the long-term best interests of the health of the company. This book helpfully analyses some of the history and current thinking on the development of the stakeholder-inclusive approach and how that can be achieved, and contributes to the debate on the purpose of a company. It also explores how the instability of corporate operations can be traced to a lack of human connectivity in the networks surrounding companies and which can be addressed in terms of mutual knowledge, alignments of interest and perceived fairness"

– Professor Mervyn King SC

"*Is Corporate Capitalism the Best We've Got to Offer?* is a timely publication that raises some compelling questions about corporate capitalism: its role as a sustainable driver for the global economy's growth, its place in a digitally-connected global market where a company can access its global customers at the click of a button, and its response to the growing demand for companies' social responsibilities. By examining the web of complicated relational issues that companies operating in this hyper-connected era face, the authors offer an insightful analysis of the relational issues and practical suggestions as to how to strengthen companies' relationships with their diverse stakeholders in order to enhance the sustainability of corporate capitalism"

**– Samuel Kwon, Chair of Global Practice,
Lee & Ko, South Korea.**

"Relational Thinking has the power to reshape the global economy. The global B Corp movement (on the demand side) and the Impact Investment movement (on the supply side) are putting relational thinking into action. This book is a timely call for all institutions systematically to apply this thinking so that we might accelerate the change – from a system of corporate capitalism that is destroying us, to a relational economic system that could restore and regenerate"

– James Perry, Co-founder & board member of B Lab UK, part of the B Corporation movement

"Corporations are often viewed and experienced as faceless and soulless institutions. We tend to forget that these are actually social constructs, invented to more effectively and efficiently organise collective human endeavour and interaction. Corporations that do not recognise and nurture their human connections and interdependencies create structural instability, not only within themselves but for the capitalist economic system as a whole as is so well argued by the authors of this book. My hope is that the guidance in this book is heeded. Challenges such as climate change and inequality are clear indications that the current paradigm is not sustainable. Companies, especially global companies, have a responsibility to be responsive to these challenges and to shift from a singular focus on profit to corporate purpose which has a more inclusive vision of value creation"

– Ansie Ramalho, Chairperson: King Committee for Corporate Governance in South Africa

"This work could not have come at a better time. It offers refreshing new perspectives on corporate capitalism that go far beyond established concerns with the current public mistrust in companies. In addition to shedding light on how stakeholder relationships influence and shape the way companies are run, the book reveals the myriad ways in which they shape how we understand and encounter the society and the world in which we live. The weakness in the relationships across these global networks is endemic. The suggested policy directions to promote mutual knowledge, alignment and fairness are indispensable"
– **Prof Arad Reisberg, Professor of Corporate Law and Finance, Head, Brunel Law School, U.K.**

"A timely book in a business world where many companies are re-examining their purpose, and considering how to relate to all their stakeholders, not just their shareholders"
– **Barbara Ridpath, Non-Executive Director in financial services companies, and Chair of the Church of England's Ethical Investment Advisory Group**

"In this bracing challenge to traditional corporate governance, Schluter demonstrates that relational stability across all stakeholders is essential to long-term corporate health. Lest their recommendations for transforming corporate enterprise seem unrealistic, they give vivid examples of companies already putting each into action. Highly recommended, even for those of us who defend shareholder-oriented governance."
– **Professor David Skeel, S. Samuel Arsht Professor of Corporate Law at the University of *Pennsylvania* Law School.**

"This book is right on the money.

Socially responsible companies depend on policy makers, customers, regulators, and stakeholders evolving their approaches alongside them, to keep in step with the urgent societal challenges we all face. Working in partnership is the only way of delivering better outcomes in an increasingly complex, interdependent world"
– **Colin Skellett, Group Chief Executive, Wessex Water**

"A fascinating book. For me the core sentence is "not approaching the human being directly but rewire national society through strategic and structural reforms". It asks people to think very differently about the fundamental role of relationships in helping individuals and societies to flourish. It raises the question of whether it is necessary to address not only the relationships but, more importantly, the conditions in which they will thrive"
– **Professor Gillian Stamp MBE, Director, Bioss the Foundation**

"The thinking of company directors has moved on from being almost exclusively focussed on shareholders, to including the interests, expectations and concerns of all major stakeholders. This book takes us one step further in the journey by demonstrating that most corporate problems can be traced to weak **human** connectivity, internally or externally, and by offering practical steps corporate leaders can take to improve connectivity through mutual knowledge, alignment of interests, and raising the level of real as well as perceived fairness in their stakeholder relationships"
– **Peter Taylor, Chairman and CEO, TTP Group plc, U.K.**

"Corporate leaders everywhere are grappling with the challenges presented by the requirements of stakeholder responsibility. Most want to do the right thing, but the inherent fuzziness of these obligations, and the temptation to manipulate them for self-interested reasons, often lead to undesirable outcomes. This book presents a coherent framework which enables leaders to confront those challenges on the basis of clear principles that are designed for the 21st century economy"
– **Lindsay Tanner, Former Federal Minister for Finance and Deregulation, Federal Government, Australia**

IS CORPORATE CAPITALISM THE BEST WE'VE GOT TO OFFER?

Books by Dr Michael Schluter CBE

- *The "R" Factor* (Hodder & Stoughton, 1993)
- *The Jubilee Manifesto* (IVP, 2005)
- *The Relational Manager* (Lion Hudson, 2009)
- *Transforming Capitalism from Within* (2011)
- *After Capitalism* (2013)
- *The Relational Lens*
  (Cambridge University Press, 2017)
- *Confederal Europe Parts 1 and 2*
  (Sallux and Jubilee Centre, 2018 and 2019)
- *Is Corporate Capitalism the Best We've Got to Offer?*
  (Relational Research, 2022)
- *No Other Way to Peace in Korea?*
  (Relational Peacebuilding Initiatives, 2022)

IS CORPORATE CAPITALISM THE BEST WE'VE GOT TO OFFER?

MICHAEL SCHLUTER

Relational Research

Relational Research
Future Business Centre, Kings Hedges Road,
Cambridge BB4 2HY, United Kingdom.
www.relationalresearch.org

ISBN 978-1-913738-67-9

Designed and typeset by Raghav Khattar

Printed and bound at Replika Press, Pvt. Ltd.

To David Lee

Friend, colleague, co-author and analyst
who helped to think through and articulate a
relational approach to public life for over 30 years

CONTENTS

LIST OF TABLES

LIST OF FIGURES

PREFACE

When Dr Schluter wrote *The R Factor* in 1993 it underpinned his vision for the launch of the Relationships Foundation which I now chair. The framework for thinking about relationships that he developed opened up two important strands of work. The first has been how factors such as time, finance, technology and culture create the conditions in which the relationships that are essential for human flourishing and organisational effectiveness are either fostered or undermined. This opens up a broad agenda for public policy and social reform that cuts across many of the traditional political divides. The second has been developing tools to measure relationships and thus inform decision-making; these have been used widely in our work to measure stakeholder relationships in both private and public sector organisations.

Both strands are evident in this book. It starts with the recognition that the social, economic and environmental consequences of the ways in which we currently practise capitalism are unsustainable. The symptoms that give rise to so much public concern include excessive pay differentials, short-termism, fraud, tax evasion, and neglect of the environment as well as both local and global communities. These, however, should not be seen primarily as individual ethical failures, but as consequences of the ways in which the complex networks of relationships around organisations have evolved. Failing to address these issues will lead to growing political disaffection, as well as demands for increased regulation, yet leaving the root causes unchecked.

The book highlights both the importance and the often-distant nature of the relationships with and between the stakeholders and networks of the company – its employees, suppliers, customers, communities, and regulators, not just its shareholders. These relationships are often strained to breaking point. Conversely, when the relationships are strong, they usually bring financial stability which in turn leads to a more stable society and politics. So, both society and government have a strong interest in the relational stability of companies.

Many important initiatives have recognised this and sought to redefine the purpose of companies, following an ESG (Environmental, Social and Governance) agenda – B Corporations, Responsible Business and the Good Business Charter for instance. If the underlying systems, however, remain relationally unstable such initiatives will only take us so far. I therefore welcome the strategy set out in this book. This includes redefining the purpose of the company so that it seeks long-term value creation for stakeholders, minimising pay differentials and the risk of financial instability through excessive debt, and treating customers, suppliers and the community fairly. The institution underpinning global capitalism, the limited liability company, has been astonishingly successful for 175 years in supporting wealth creation. To those who argue that the free market – and its foremost institution, the company – should be left alone, the book counters that limited liability is an extraordinary benefit granted by law which demands extraordinary responsibility to society.

Adopting such a strategy still depends upon the willingness of investors to do so, underlining their disproportionate power. Such voluntary initiatives will also be challenging if the overall business environment works against them. Governments and parliaments therefore have a vital role to play in making targeted interventions that support relational stability and hence sustainable wealth creation. Implementing such a strategy will require companies to measure and manage all their relationships more effectively. Again, the book sets out ways in which this can be done.

I hope this book will attract wide attention, and will contribute to reform of corporate governance and management in a way which satisfies those with either left-wing or right-wing leanings – and thus serve as a unifying vision in our increasingly divided Western societies. For our part, we will continue to make the case that governments, companies and public services should recognise the importance of relationships and seek to create the conditions that allow them to flourish. We will also continue to develop and promote the tools and dashboards that empower people to put good intentions into practice.

– Jeremy Lefroy FCA,
Chair of Trustees, Relationships Foundation, Cambridge UK,
Member of Parliament for Stafford, UK (2010–2019),
Co-Founder of the Equity for Africa Group of companies

FOREWORD

It is now over twenty years since I first worked with the author on ways to support organisations in the management of their key relationships through better measurement. The focus then was on the more immediate, visible relationships that were significant performance and risk factors. This book looks at the wider and often less visible network of relationships in which all organisations sit. These have widened and, the author argues, become less stable as investors, customers, suppliers and other stakeholders have become increasingly connected digitally and through intermediaries. This book is timely and important. Timely because we have seen how events such banking crises, Brexit, the Covid-19 pandemic and now, at the time of writing, war in Ukraine have all in different ways revealed both our reliance on the complex networks of business, trade and finance but also their risks and fragility. Important, because despite the growing commitment to sustainability and corporate social responsibility, the evidence of relational instability remains all too evident. Discontent with the way capitalism works continues to be fuelled by corporate scandals, excessive director pay, industrial disputes, short-termism, harm to the environment, fraud, tax-evasion, or cronyism.

I have sat in many board meetings with all the attendant financial, performance, ESG and other reports. We know that the words and numbers represent the outcomes of interactions between many stakeholders, some well-known and visible, and many whom few if any people in the company will ever meet or know. Good policies and practice are important in managing this challenge, and this book offers many welcome examples of how companies across the globe have done this. A key message of the book, however, is that the problems we see are not simply the result of individual choices and priorities but are shaped by systemically-embedded rules and structures that weaken human connectivity between key stakeholders, directors, employees, communities, suppliers and investors.

There are some simple truths about good business, not least the need for clarity of purpose and good data on how it is being achieved. Building on the foundation that the purpose of companies should be 'to serve society through long-term value creation in the interests of all its major stakeholders, while honouring wider responsibilities to society and the environment', the book offers a useful litmus test for an organisation's network of relationships:

1. **Do they know each other?** How far does the network embody direct, durable, diverse interaction, including necessary information flows?
2. **Are basic goals aligned?** How far does the network embody a congruence of values and goals, including rules governing competition?
3. **Is this arrangement fair?** How far does the network embody a balance of fairness for all parties, including future generations?

The ability to give good answers to these questions is a good indicator of whether companies are well placed to navigate the risks they face. The rewards are tangible and are likely to be seen in such areas as employee motivation, productivity, cost-effectiveness, quality of service, reputation, brand value and ultimately share value. But the challenge is not for companies alone. As governments around the world seek to address the challenges of debt, inequality, climate change and wellbeing they will need to create the conditions in which companies can prosper and be part of the solution.

– Shonaid Jemmett-Page,
Independent Non-executive Director, Aviva plc,
Chair of Greencoat UK Wind plc as well as of Cordiant
Digital Infrastructure Limited,
Senior Independent Director of ClearBank Limited,
Independent Non-Executive Director of QinetiQ Group plc

EXECUTIVE SUMMARY

The main thesis of this book

The crucial importance of stakeholder relationships is now widely recognised. However, in practice, global companies rely not just on face-to-face interaction with their stakeholders but on digital communication with their networks, for example, with global supply chains and complex interconnected groups of suppliers and customers. So effective relationships in these huge networks are crucially important, which depends in turn on the human connectivity of these networks. Consequently, the major challenge facing us is not simply about ethics: rather it is to design companies and markets, as well as governments, in such a way that the pursuit of wealth, justice and sustainability does not become self-defeating.

The second key issue to increase public acceptability and financial stability of Corporate Capitalism is the need to realign corporate stakeholder relationship priorities, which currently give excessive attention to the interests of shareholders over all other major stakeholders who are impacted by its values and behaviour. The starting point of this book is a simple proposition: that if we are serious about transforming Corporate Capitalism, whether Western Capitalism or "State Capitalism"[1], we will need to start by looking at how these systems connect us as human beings. This is especially important in periods of a global pandemic, or political, environmental or financial turbulence. At the same time, the purpose of companies will need to be redefined so that the four major stakeholder groups of employees, customers, suppliers, and shareholders, as well as the need to honour wider responsibilities to local and global communities and the environment, are all given equal weight in decisions of directors. Of special importance are the "global communities" which companies have the opportunity to influence. Through their engagement, they can increase the incomes and welfare of millions in low-income countries in Africa, South and South Asia, Latin America and the Middle East where most of the 9 per cent of the world population who live in extreme poverty can be found today.[2]

Much of institutional apparatus embodied in Corporate Capitalism today is unfit for purpose because it is blind to the way such connections actually work. In today's global society, few relationships are personal. Instead, we are linked *en masse* through vast, complex networks (financial, political, social, digital) whose shape and rules of engagement exert a powerful influence on behaviour while being, wholly or partly, beyond individual control. How we treat one another at a global level, and how effectively we cooperate in social and environmental crises, is to a significant degree a question of what behaviours these mass links incentivise.

Figure 1. The impact of strong human connectivity for companies.

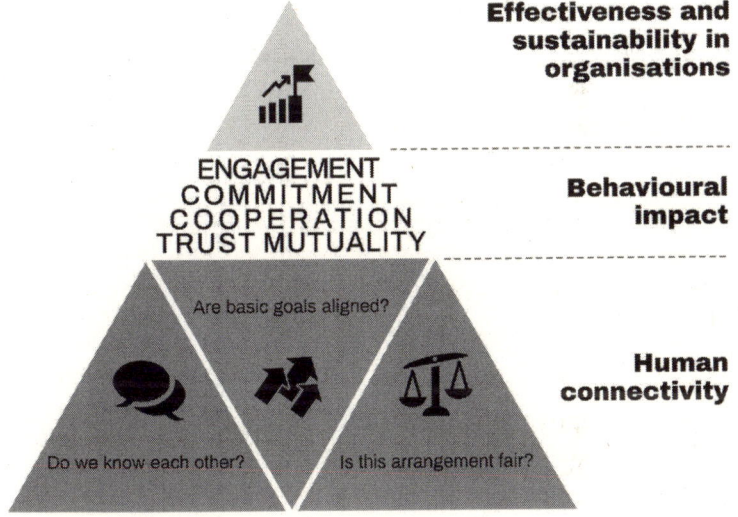

The book's core model is shown in Figure 1. Numerous studies have explored the connection between organisational effectiveness/sustainability and prosocial behaviours – engagement, commitment, trust, cooperation, and mutuality. But these behaviours do not exist in isolation. They are fostered by a property inherent in the networks out of which markets, companies and governments are constructed – namely, *human connectivity*.

Even in a network with millions of members, we can ask three key questions of its constituent individuals or stakeholder groups:

1. **Do they know each other?** How far does the network embody direct, durable, diverse interaction, including necessary information flows?
2. **Are basic goals aligned?** How far does the network embody a congruence of values and goals, including rules governing competition?
3. **Is this arrangement fair?** How far does the network embody a balance of fairness for all parties, including future generations?

The better a network connects its members, the stronger and more effective their cooperation is likely to be. Conversely, if barriers to transparency mean people are insufficiently present to one another, if the network fails to align their goals, and if the arrangements binding them together are perceived as unfair, the network itself will tend towards weakness, conflict and disintegration. The relationships it creates will not sustain it. It will be *relationally unstable.*

At present, Corporate Capitalism does not ensure that the interests of all stakeholders are properly considered in strategic decisions, nor that stakeholder relationships and their wider network relationships have the necessary relational stability, and thus the resilience required for financial sustainability, which in turn undergirds national political stability – especially in democratic societies.

The need for relational stability forces us to ask the question: *What is this company here to do?* Like it or not, a company relies on the effort, resources and goodwill of a diverse group of stakeholders, all of whom have at least a moral claim on how this accumulation of financial power is used. The peculiar construction of the listed company, with its current explicit or implicit bias to shareholders, has introduced a relational instability with widespread and sometimes conflicting effects. It requires closer examination.

Business and relational instability

In a business context, the evidence of relational instability makes for familiar reading: corporate scandals, excessive director pay, industrial disputes, worker disengagement, short-termism, careless practice, harm to the environment, fraud, tax-evasion, and reputational damage.

The reflex response is to blame dysfunction on individuals – the rogue director, the pressurised manager. But in the context of weak human connectivity, destructive behaviours in a company are not simple ethical failures. Rather, they are catalysed by institutionally-embedded rules and structures that weaken human connectivity between key stakeholders – directors, employees, consumers, suppliers and investors.

There are three reasons why business should treat relational instability as a source of risk.

First, because relational instability impacts directly on key aspects of company performance, including employee motivation, productivity, cost-effectiveness, profitability, quality of service, reputation, brand value and ultimately share value. Second, because a relationally unstable company will be less resilient to the kind of shocks that are increasingly part of the global landscape in which companies have to operate. And third, because relational instability is more than a vague intangible: it can be measured.

A detailed plan for mitigating relational instability through a Relational Stability Strategy takes up the middle section of the book. The first and essential part of this strategy is to redefine the purpose of companies as to serve society through long-term value creation in the interests of all its major stakeholders, while honouring wider responsibilities to local communities and the environment. This is not about tick-box compliance with ESG (Environmental, Social and Governance) criteria, but about the rules and conditions companies establish across their entire networks of stakeholders – how much mutual knowledge really exists; how well-aligned objectives really are; and whether all those involved in the network can say that its arrangements are acceptably fair. Any business can build relational stability, even if it is listed on multiple exchanges, and examples are given of companies, among them major global corporates, who have successfully implemented some of the recommended measures, even if in a fragmentary way.

Relational instability and public policy

The years since the financial crisis of 2008 have seen a surge of initiatives designed to leverage concern and goodwill both among company directors and the fund managers who influence them (for example, B Corporations, Responsible Business and the Good Business Charter).

The problem such initiatives face in attempting to repurpose capitalism is that relational instability in companies is intimately linked to relational instability in surrounding political and social structures. These include core philosophical foundations that promote individual choice or state control above the network relationships that enable both individuals and societies to flourish.

In the corporate world, this means that primary institutions like markets, and primary financial arrangements like limited liability, have been designed in such a way that wealth creation and social-environmental responsibility quickly come into conflict. More widely, it triggers a range of negative feedback loops affecting the national interest, including the gradual erosion of social support systems, a decline in tax-paying working-age populations, budgetary strains on welfare and healthcare, political polarisation, and systemic risks incurred by debt-burdened consumers, companies and nations.

For this reason, the concluding section of the book examines the role of government in tackling relational instability not just in companies but across society generally. There are three reasons why this may be advantageous:

1. It provides a language with which company directors, investors and government together can navigate an increasingly challenging phase of social change.

2. Since social and environmental problems are to a large extent a secondary effect of relational instability in economic, political and digital networks, it provides a way to address causes systematically.

3. By drawing attention to the incentivising power of networks, it relies not on turning business or political leaders into ethical pioneers but on establishing the preconditions for ethical behaviour in systems and infrastructure.

In the end, both capitalism and democracy are relational constructs. That is, they arrange sets of stakeholder groups in particular configurations. Some of these are very large. Around those configurations, are created rules, customs, and protocols by which the resulting mass relationships are organised and managed. Neither Right nor Left has paid much attention to the way such networks operate. Doing so now may be the key to a globally sustainable and prosperous future.

> "*Society is demanding that companies, both public and private, serve a social purpose. To prosper over time, every company must not only deliver financial performance, but also show how it makes a positive contribution to society. Companies must benefit all of their stakeholders, including shareholders, employees, customers, and the communities in which they operate.*"

LARRY FINK,
chairman and chief executive of BlackRock,
the world's biggest investor,
in his annual letter to CEOs, 2019[3]

1. INTRODUCTION

Ten years before the arrival of Covid-19, corporate leaders were already coming around to the view that the economic system needed fixing.

For many years the default position of US (and, in a more diluted form, global) capitalism had been the one articulated by economist Milton Friedman in 1970: "There is one and only one social responsibility of business – to engage in activities designed to increase its profits." Or, as the American Business Roundtable added in its 1997 statement of purpose, "The interests of other stakeholders are relevant as a derivative of the duty to stockholders."

What had changed the game was 2008. Global markets went into meltdown in a particularly dramatic and public way. A shockwave of economic calamity circled the planet. Massive state support introduced a decade of recession and stagnating wages, for which few were held to account. And into the middle of this economic maelstrom dropped, first, the realisation that human occupancy of the planet can no longer ignore its environmental impact, and second, a global pandemic. In all of this, an attitudinal shift is occurring – particularly among the young. A 2016 Harvard study showed that over half (51 per cent) of Americans between the ages of 18 and 29 "did not support capitalism". A *Fortune*/NP Strategy poll in 2019 showed that 80 per cent of 18–24-year-olds want to work for "engaged companies". As Johnson & Johnson CEO Alex Gorsky put it, "People are asking fundamental questions about how well capitalism is serving society."

In December 2018, *Fortune* took up an invitation from Pope Francis to bring a hundred top CEOs to Rome and spend a day figuring out how companies could help solve global social problems. That the meeting took place at all is, of course, encouraging, and what happened in that discussion fits into a larger narrative where influential voices have looked for some additional ingredient that will make capitalism palatable. It should be – as various commentators have suggested – "compassionate" (Mark Benioff), "inclusive" (Lynn Forester de Rothschild), "sustaining" (Conference Board research group) or represent "shared value" (John Mackey).

The question is whether, in practice, all this soul-searching produces any more than what social critic Anand Giridharadas calls "virtuous side hustles".[4]

Companies are unique in the type and degree of influence they wield.[5] They are the main economic bedrock in many countries and form the background of capitalist systems. Almost everywhere in advanced economies they are the principal means by which wealth is created (with a significant multiplier effect on employment). We rely on them to supply us with food, clothes, household goods, medicines, transportation, energy, vacations, entertainment, banking services, consumer credit and mortgages.

They also have an enormous collateral impact on culture and society, affecting employment, educational priorities, hours worked, dietary and lifestyle choices, and willingness to take on consumer debt. They have changed the way we work, the way we interact, the way we shop, and the way we use our leisure time. In some cases, their sheer size gives them leverage over public policy (through corporate lobbying) and over electoral outcomes (by making substantial campaign contributions and, more recently, through the impact of a few corporates on social media networks). Their political connections can – as in the recent case of Chinese telecommunications giant Huawei – raise questions of national security. Their activities and products help to drive consumer/public attitudes, for example on treatment of waste and use of plastics, and government decisions on use of coal for power stations which also drive climate change.

As a result, companies have a complex relationship with their surrounding stakeholders. As engines of financial wealth generation, they are unsurpassed: in his book *Firm Commitment*, Colin Mayer calls the modern corporation "a miracle and one of the most ingenious concepts ever devised".[6] At the same time, as social assets, companies are often dysfunctional – because the immense power they can exercise and profits they can generate are not bound to serve the interests of all those affected by their actions, including those who rely on them for a living.

The stakes are high. As Edward Freeman notes, "If we continue to divorce Wall Street from Main Street, we can expect a populist revolt that may harm the very idea of capitalism as free people cooperating together to create value for each other."[7]

This book argues that the faults of capitalism, so often laid at the door of big-company CEOs, are in fact a product of particular properties that have, often inadvertently, been baked into the networks out of which companies and markets (and much else) are constructed, and through which they have to operate. If we want to solve the problems of Corporate Capitalism, we will have to redesign those networks to have different characteristics. We will have to make them more relationally stable. We will also need to reset the purpose of companies to reorder their relationship priorities with stakeholders and thereby increase their public acceptability.

2. WHAT IS RELATIONAL INSTABILITY?

Analysing corporate misconduct, it is tempting to put blame in the wrong place.

In 2010, the blowout at BP's Deepwater Horizon oil rig in the Gulf of Mexico cost eleven lives and caused the largest marine oil spill in US history. The estimated 4.9-million-barrel spillage affected livelihoods along at least 1,300 miles of coastline[8] and kick-started a chain of environmental impacts associated with the release of the oil and the use of dispersants to clear it.

Five years later, the United States Environmental Protection Agency determined that Volkswagen had installed software on 11 million diesel cars which activated emissions controls only during laboratory emissions testing. In real driving conditions, the same cars could produce up to forty times the legal emissions limit.[9]

In both cases, investigations were launched to determine what had gone wrong and who was responsible. But behind all this lies a convenient assumption. Although a company may, in legal terms, be liable for damages caused by its operations, much of the scrutiny focuses on the actions and motives of the people who run it. This is convenient because individual bad actors (incompetent managers, overpaid executives) provide good copy for the media and can be dismissed, prosecuted, or otherwise purged from the system without provoking more difficult questions. For example, why does the Anglo-American model of capitalism seem more volatile than others, or why have companies everywhere appeared to be more directly sensitive to threats endangering profitability than they are to issues of wider societal or environmental wellbeing.

The assertion put forward in this book is that the moral and leadership quality of individual office-holders does not provide a total, or even adequate, explanation of corporate misconduct, or indeed of any other weakness in the market economy. The real problem with companies lies in the way they fail to connect people, because companies, like governments, cities and social media, fundamentally consist of large networks of people bound together in complex sets of relationships. How those people are connected determines not only how they are likely to behave but also the sustainability and long-term competitive advantage of the company.

How relational instability arises

It is often said that a successful team or organisation adds up to more than the sum of its parts.

The intangibles that contribute to this success (trust, engagement, commitment, generosity, loyalty, altruism) make a familiar list and are generally regarded as forming the essential social capital on which business is built. How they can be conjured into existence among those who make up a company, organisation or institution has long been debated both by business leaders and academics. Features like trust and engagement in a network only emerge, however, if certain catalytic qualities are *present in the network itself*. Looking at a collection of individuals or stakeholder groups, we should ask three questions about the way a network brings people together:

1. **Do they know each other?** How far does the network embody direct, durable, diverse interaction, including necessary information flows?
2. **Are basic goals aligned?** How far does the network embody a congruence of values and goals, including rules governing competition?
3. **Is this arrangement fair?** How far does the network embody a balance of fairness for all parties, including future generations?

If people can't easily know one another, if the network fails to align their goals, and if the arrangements binding them together are perceived as unfair, the network will not have the capacity to outperform. Rather the opposite. It will tend towards fragmentation, conflict and disintegration. It will be relationally unstable.

> *Relational instability can be defined as that property of a network – specifically the degree to which its rules, protocols and structure limit mutual knowledge, alignment and fairness – which makes network members less visible to one another as human beings and less strongly incentivised to cooperate.*[10]

Of course, the ability to know others, the ability to set goals, and the ability to judge fairness, all reside in the individual or stakeholder group. A network, though, adds two sets of variables that are distinctively its own. First, it will possess structural characteristics (hard factors like location, transport connection and IT) which influence how people meet and interact. And second, it will hold inside it rules, protocols, customs, traditions and habits that either were imposed on the network at its formation or will have become established within it over years of use.[11]

In small, informal networks, individuals generally make their own rules. In larger ones – schools, hospitals, social media networks, companies, nations – member control over rules is limited. Nevertheless, both the structure of the network and its rules exert a powerful influence over behaviour. Societies of all kinds contain sociopaths, but it is the nature of social media platforms as networks (the structure that brings large numbers of strangers together and the rules governing user anonymity and the use of avatars) that creates the phenomenon of trolling.

The impact of networks on behaviour is recognisably the same across time and culture, and Table 1 explores the three variables in more detail. Because human connectivity is nearly always easier to establish at a small scale (teams, local clubs, families, neighbourhoods),[12] it is tempting to assume that small must always be beautiful. But this isn't true.

For example, in fourteenth-century England most traditional communities were small. Locally there were often high levels of mutual knowledge. But the interests of landowners were at variance with those of artisans, tenant farmers and agricultural labourers, as well as the urban working classes. And it was perceived unfairness, signalled by attempts to impose the poll tax and fix maximum wages during the labour shortage following the Black Death, that pushed an already relationally unstable society into its first general uprising – Wat Tyler's Rebellion of 1381.[13]

Over six centuries later, the people and the institutions have changed, but the dynamics of relational instability – both as a risk created by weak human connectivity and as an organisational state vulnerable to external shocks – remains the same, affecting everything from companies to nations to international cooperation. In fact, through the economic advances of the last two hundred years (and the digital revolution of the last thirty) relational instability has emerged on a scale never seen before.

The main reason is a step-change in the sheer number of relationships modern institutions generate. Pre-industrial societies relied on relatively sparse networks linked together by personal contact and a limited number of physical records. In today's high-income societies, by contrast, the vast majority of our relationships, including those on which the political economy relies, no longer depend on personal interaction. Rather they are created, *ex nihilo,* by the institutions that join us together. Each of us stands at the centre of a vast penumbra of these relationships. Typically, they incorporate us *en masse* as members of a class or stakeholder group (consumer, saver, investor, employee, voter, follower), binding us into wider society less through the exercising of personal initiative than through bulk arrangements embedded in the economy, social structure, media environment and political order. According to estimates by the World Economic Forum, the resulting data trail will reach 463 exabytes (equivalent to over 200 million DVDs) per day by 2025.[14]

Broadly, if only in specific ways, this has boosted human connectivity. Thanks to search engines and social media, we enjoy in-depth, real-time access to much of the global knowledge base. We are more quickly and keenly aware of the plight of other world citizens affected by natural disaster or political repression. We better understand the interdependency of the world and the depth of humanity's impact on the planetary commons. Also, some innovations in IT, like blockchain, succeed precisely because they generate new frameworks for mutual knowledge, alignment and fairness.

At the same time, the scale of global organisation opens up vast human connectivity gaps that undermine effective joint action. Despite the IT revolution we remain a global community of strangers. Even the concerted and widely-advertised threat of global warming has produced only limited alignment between nations which are simultaneously trying to retain their advantage in geopolitics and fossil-fuel-based global markets. The EU's perceived failure to build adequate fairness and accountability into its political structures has resulted in the withdrawal of the UK amid a wider drift towards nationalism and rights-based identity politics. More widely, the institutions that support global capitalism and governance have failed to overhaul an economic model that for two centuries has created mass relationships less concerned with the risks of relational instability than with the narrow goals of wealth creation and, frequently, maintaining the vested interests of ruling regimes.

In a low-human-connectivity environment, control typically shifts away from members and towards the institutions that run or regulate the networks. Hence the account management tools provided by a bank to its customers increase convenience but allow little room for negotiation over credit rating, overdraft limits or rates of interest. Social media giants happily multiply user accounts and exploit user data, but are notoriously deaf to customer complaints. Examples abound of government interventions to control social made networks. In December 2019, internet and text messaging services were suspended by order of the Indian government in an attempt to tackle unrest with a communications clampdown.[15] The Chinese government continues to practise extensive internet censorship, effectively silencing many of China's most critical voices advocating reform.[16]

The accelerating pace of IT encourages institutions to reduce relationships themselves to data – usually in a quest for accuracy and speed. Algorithms trade the stock market and vet job applications; FAQs displace customer phone lines; markets and electorates are predictively segmented to receive targeted messaging; feedback is herded into online comment boxes; online data entry pervades multiple functions from e-commerce to filling out tax returns. Across big networks, a gap opens up between actuality and perception, allowing individuals (including celebrities and political leaders) to build carefully-crafted media identities, while the space that should belong to mutual knowledge instead becomes dominated by tribal animosities, internet scams, and conspiracy theories.

Nevertheless, these vast social, political and economic networks are not mere abstractions. They represent actual relations including the exercise of enormous power and influence, between actual people. So, the fact that they tend to be relationally unstable should concern us. If successful economies and their sustainability depend on fostering cooperation, engagement and commitment among stakeholders, then a systematic tendency to weaken human connectivity creates risk.

There are three reasons why businesses, in particular, should take this risk seriously.

First, relational instability impacts directly on key aspects of company performance, including productivity, cost-effectiveness, profitability, quality of service, reputation, brand value and collectively on company valuation.

Table 1. The three interrelated variables of human connectivity.

Variable	Network Property	Explanation
MUTUAL KNOWLEDGE	*How far the network embodies direct, durable, diverse interaction, including necessary information flows*	More than any other element, mutual knowledge drives empathy, enriching mutual encounter and cementing experience into shared history. But it also implies an appropriate balance of privacy, transparency and accountability, and underlies the quality and directness of information flows. In complex organisations, it is about the visibility of key data, the avoidance of groupthink, and recruiting and promoting people with the right skills.
ALIGNMENT	*How far the network embodies congruence of values and goals, including rules governing competition*	Alignment is the necessary foundation of non-coercive cooperation. It matters in complex societies because vital and intensely competitive processes (markets, tendering, job applications, resource allocation, elections, parliamentary debate, law courts, Premiership football) only work if they operate within a set of agreed values, objectives and rules.
FAIRNESS	*How far the network embodies a balance of fairness for all parties, including future generations*	Fairness in networks, including respect in the way parties are acknowledged and represented, strongly motivates participation. It permeates the just imposition of law in the forms of thoroughness and impartiality. Economically, it implies a consideration of the young and those not yet born who will often bear the consequences of current decisions. Systemically, it holds within it the foundation of the rights and responsibilities of both individuals and organisations in networks.

Second, a relationally unstable company will be less resilient to the kind of shocks that are increasingly part of the landscape in which companies have to operate. Some of these shocks are natural and effectively unavoidable – extreme weather events, volcanic eruptions, earthquakes, pandemics. Others – like economic downturns, shifts in commodity prices or consumer demand or interest rates, imposition of tariffs, changes of government, or the emergence of disruptive new technologies – are closely linked to political and economic cycles. Still others, some of which we will return to later in the book, result directly or indirectly from relational instability embedded in political and financial systems. Among these are Brexit, market volatility, the financial crisis of 2008, regional conflicts, and several major industrial accidents. Whatever the cause of the shocks, company resilience will depend in large measure on the relational stability of its networks.

A combination of factors makes the twenty-first century unusually hazardous both for companies and states. More than ever before, humanity is testing the limits of environmental tolerance at a planetary level. Advances in IT and engineering allow us to build complex supply chains[17] that increase personal choice and quality of life for the better-off but simultaneously reduce local economic resilience and leave essential national systems vulnerable to disruption. No country can be sealed off from a virus or an economic crisis or a cyber-attack. Meanwhile artificial intelligence is redefining the purpose and scope of human labour, creating both a new technological elite and new realms of redundancy, while growth feeds on global consumption which in turn feeds the accumulation of global debt. It has never been more important to facilitate cooperation – and yet the limits to cooperation imposed by relational instability remain largely unacknowledged and unexplored.

The third reason businesses should take relational instability seriously is that it can be measured and reported on. Table 2 shows the diagnostic framework such metrics follow. Note again that the focus is not on individual behaviour but on the structure, rules and customs a corporation imposes on or accepts in the networks that surround and compose it – not least because structure, rules and customs are under the control, or require the permission of, company directors in a way that individual behaviour does not.

Note also that the picture will be complex. Evaluating relational instability encompasses more than just the relationship between management and workforce. A company's networks connect a range of stakeholders, internal and external, and the assessment of fairness, in particular, will involve a judgment as to whether one interface in the network (for example, between directors and investors) is advantaged at the expense of another (for example, between directors and workforce). See Appendix 1 for more details.

Table 2. Measurement of the three variables
that constitute human connectivity.

Question	Variable	Network Property	Sample of Diagnostics
Do they know one another?	MUTUAL KNOWLEDGE	*How far the network embodies direct, durable, diverse interaction, including necessary information flows*	• Does the network facilitate means by which stakeholders can know and understand one another's perspectives? • What rules govern how often, by what means, for how long, and over what period stakeholders can meet or interact – including the content of those interactions? • What value is placed on durable personal acquaintance between those on either end of a crucial inter-organisational relationship? • Does the network strike an acceptable balance between ensuring transparency and respecting privacy? • Do cross-cutting relationships exist to link different stakeholder groups?
Are basic goals aligned?	ALIGNMENT	*How far the network embodies a congruence of values and goals, including rules governing competition*	• At what points are the values of all stakeholders already aligned? • Are underlying shared values articulated in the company mission and values statements, does it know the values of other companies in its multi-company network? • How clearly are company values communicated and how actively are they supported?

			• Are employees, suppliers, customers and investors involved in the effort to build aligned values?
			• What rules exist for constructively managing competitive processes?
Is this arrangement fair?	FAIRNESS	*How far the network embodies a balance of fairness for all parties, including future generations*	• Would arrangements be deemed fair to all stakeholders by a neutral third party?
			• Does a majority of people or organisations in each stakeholder group believe the arrangement is fair?
			• Are all parties accorded the same treatment and respect?
			• Are dissenting voices heard and acknowledged?
			• Are all significantly-affected stakeholder groups represented in the making of key decisions?
			• Does the company's overall mission support global efforts toward sustainability?

3. WHY LISTED COMPANIES ARE OFTEN RELATIONALLY UNSTABLE

The relationship between company directors and investors in the company is one of the most powerful and is particularly significant in listed companies. Although not the most numerous as a category, companies whose shares are listed on one or more stock exchanges are by far the largest and most wealthy at a global level. At the end of June 2021, the total market capitalisation of US public companies alone stood at $47 trillion.[18]

Origins of the listed company model

No two listed companies are identical, and the structures of larger ones are often highly complex, consisting of a parent with numerous operating and other subsidiaries which may be spread across several countries. Nevertheless, all companies tend to have similar stakeholder ecosystems. These are shown in simplified schematic form in Figure 2.

The distinction between investors and directors goes back at least as far as AD 1250, when 96 shares of the Société des Moulins du Bazacle in France's Garonne valley were traded at a value that depended on the profitability of the company's mills. Shares became tradable on an exchange for the first time when the Dutch East India Company issued shares and bonds, having been established in 1602 on being granted a monopoly over Dutch operations in Asia by the States-General of the Netherlands. Participating investors shared at least two interests: start-up costs (in this case, construction, fitting out and manning of vessels, as well as funding the company's other significant operations) and risk – not inconsiderable, as many ships that headed round the Cape of Good Hope simply never returned, although in this case shareholder risk was limited to the amount of their investment in the company.

Incorporation in the UK was an expensive privilege granted by the state, either by Royal Charter, creating a chartered company, or by private Act of Parliament, creating a statutory company. It has been suggested that in principle this meant that a company was incorporated with public good objectives in mind.[19] It perhaps also reflected an alignment of interest between investors, entrepreneurs and the community at large. The Bank of England, for instance, was established in 1694 both by Royal Charter and Act of Parliament, its purpose as decreed by the Charter being to "promote the public good and benefit our people."

*Figure 2. Simplified schematic model of
stakeholder relationships in a listed company.*

Note that the subsidiaries, which are wholly or partly owned by the parent company, will each have their own stakeholders.

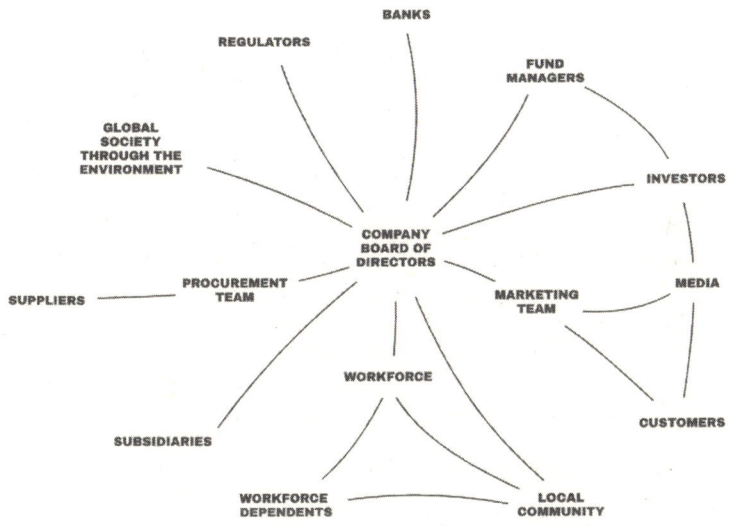

Early companies were usually formed to develop trade with new colonies and later for infrastructure at home (including utilities, railways and canals). Devices to gain the benefit of company status without being incorporated included forming partnerships to make them as similar as possible to chartered and statutory companies. Company formation became easier with the UK's Joint Stock Companies Act 1844 which allowed companies to be created by simple registration. However, shareholders continued to have personal liability for the company's debts if it failed and, while this tended to make them advocate prudence and caution, it also had the effect of disincentivising investment and restraining economic growth.

The solution was legislation, first enacted by the State of New York in 1811, which limited the liability of shareholders to the amount of their investment in the company. Britain's Limited Liability Act was passed by Parliament in 1855.

Limited companies were, in legal terms, not much different from a person – but a person potentially immortal and endowed with power and benefits few individuals could ever hold. A share in a company was no longer an equitable interest in its assets but rather a residual claim on its future profits.[20] Shareholders generally had no responsibility for the actions of directors or for the company's liabilities were it to fail. The most they could lose was the value of their shares.

The notion of a private legal entity, with a separate legal personality distinct from its directors and shareholders, which could enter into contracts, could sue and be sued in its own right, could own assets, borrow funds, raise share capital and could outlive the people running it, was striking and had almost no historical precedent. And thanks to the de-risking of investment through limiting the liability of shareholders, what followed was a massive injection of private capital into business. By the end of the nineteenth century, most European nations had enacted similar laws, and the limited liability model, with its unique method of amassing finance, has dominated the capitalist landscape ever since. The West's economic engine had been fired up.

Human connectivity tends to decrease as companies and their surrounding stakeholder groups grow larger. The development of share trading markets has tended to isolate the directors who run a company from those who own its shares. Moreover, the directors who control and manage an enterprise have become distinct from the employees hired to run it. In the nineteenth century, this separation, often reinforced by steep differentials of wealth and power, solidified into class-based differences of interest that played into the wider relational instabilities of politics and society.

Both the Wall Street Crash of 1929 and the financial crisis of 2008 arose directly from the relational instabilities inherent in listed companies and the financial markets that support them, under the analysis put forward by this book. The first triggered a global recession and encouraged the rise of German National Socialism. We are still living in the shadow of the second. Meanwhile, although both companies and capitalism have changed significantly over the years, their relational instabilities have not gone away – only taken new and, in some respects, more dangerous forms.

We shall now apply the human connectivity test to the stakeholder issues outlined above, with their enormous consequences for the success and sustainability of companies:

Question 1: Do they know one another?

How far does the network embody direct, durable, diverse interaction, including necessary information flows?

Mutual knowledge between stakeholders is crucial to building cooperation. Yet, as indicated in Figure 3, mutual knowledge is likely to be unevenly distributed across a company's stakeholder network. CEOs and other executives will have regular interaction with senior managers. Similarly, a workforce will be strongly integrated with family and local community. But in larger companies it is rare for these two groups to overlap. Nor are CEOs and other executives likely to be well-acquainted with rank-and-file investors.

This hasn't always been the case. A hundred years ago it was not unusual for shareholders to participate in the life of the company as if they were part of a shared endeavour. According to the *New York Times*, one shareholder in the Canada Life Insurance Company attended 65 successive annual meetings.[21] On the front page of the 25 October 1917 issue of the *Wall Street Journal*, a report was published about the annual meeting of the New Haven Railroad. The proceedings were lively, and "in spite of a heavy downpour" the meeting was "packed as usual with stockholders". One stockholder by the name of Walter Leigh even made a motion to open the meeting with a prayer "For us all and the New Haven Railroad in particular".[22]

Figure 3. Schematic model of stakeholder relationships in a listed company, showing interfaces where mutual knowledge is likely to be highest. The thickness of the line indicates the degree of mutual knowledge.

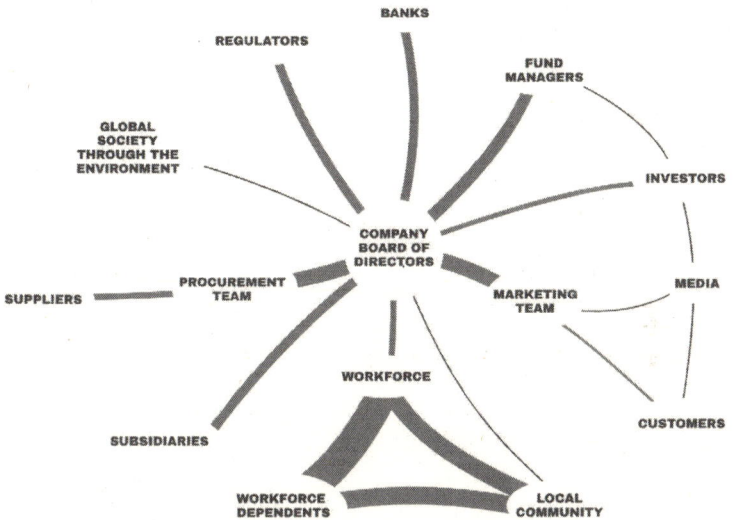

Today, most listed companies show far less interest in engaging with smaller shareholders, although they would expect regular meetings with a few larger shareholders, for instance fund managers. Numbers of shareholders are generally much larger than in the past. And because companies tend to be separated from capital providers by the labyrinthine intermediation of the financial markets, directors cannot know with certainty, from one moment to the next, who actually owns many of the company's shares.[23] Nor can the capital providers easily answer the question as to where exactly their capital is invested if, for instance, they invest through professionally-managed funds. In France's tradition of interlocking share ownership between companies, the model of a distinct company with distinct shareholders fails extensively.

Modern shareholding is baffling in its complexity. Investors in unit trusts and managed funds, for instance, do not actually own shares in listed companies; rather they have a financial interest in a fund which will itself have an interest in numerous individual companies, often in a variety of countries. Similarly, the pension fund for a final salary scheme isn't actually held by the employees and pensioners at all, but by the fund trustees. They will usually place it under the control of a fund manager (often from a different company) tasked with investing not directly in companies but in other funds which themselves invest and deal in companies' shares. And that's leaving aside derivatives and the crowd of other investment products that make up today's financial marketplace.

Some individual investors do still attend AGMs and EGMs, but even here the directors' closest links with the investing community are likely to be through fund managers, whose control of large blocks of voting rights often gives them a considerable degree of influence over the appointment of directors and the approval of remuneration packages. Direct feedback from shareholders has largely been overtaken by the ubiquitous presence of social media which companies, like governments, can use but not control.

More widely, the revolutions in transportation and telecommunications have generally raised levels of mutual knowledge across company networks. For example, the climate change debate, catalysed by social media, represents a step up in mutual knowledge between investors and the stakeholder groups most affected by company operations. Underlying commonalities arising from sharing one finite planet become acutely obvious, and the result is a rising wave of shareholder activism. Companies in the US faced a record number of climate-related shareholder proposals at their 2019 shareholder meetings[24] and pressure on boardrooms to increase contact further by being transparent about climate change risk[25] – a move that no doubt played its part in 101 US corporations pledging in 2019 to become carbon neutral.[26]

Within companies, some important innovations in work practices have involved deliberately shortening lines of communication. *Nemawashi* in Japan means discussing a decision in advance with relevant stakeholders – not only to secure consensus but also to ensure that all perspectives are looked at with a view to making the decision itself better. In developing the Lexus, its entry into the luxury car market, Toyota set up an *obeya* (literally a large room) where everything relevant to the development could be displayed (including schedules, design graphics, manpower charts and financial status) as a work-base for the chief engineer and their key personnel.[27] Data dashboards and online project management systems like Basecamp, Asana and Trello try to exploit the same benefits of a global view and facilitated interaction.

Question 2: Are basic goals aligned?

How far does the network embody a congruence of values and goals, including rules governing competition?

A typical company brings together large numbers of people who connect with it for quite different reasons. Those reasons may not align. In a supermarket chain, the interests of customers, who want cheap milk, can easily conflict with the interests of farmers, who may be struggling to keep dairy herds economically viable. Governments benefit from companies' ability to provide employment and contribute to the national exchequer, while companies may find their financial interests best served by directing their profits to low-tax regimes. From the viewpoint of investors, the goals of employees (job security, a decent wage, reasonable hours) or of suppliers (being paid on time, not having profit margins squeezed) may only register as a profit-threatening cost on the profit and loss account.

The colours on Figure 4 represent the contrasting interests of the different stakeholder groups within a listed company's network.

Figure 4. Schematic model of stakeholder relationships in a listed company, showing the variety of interests present across the network.

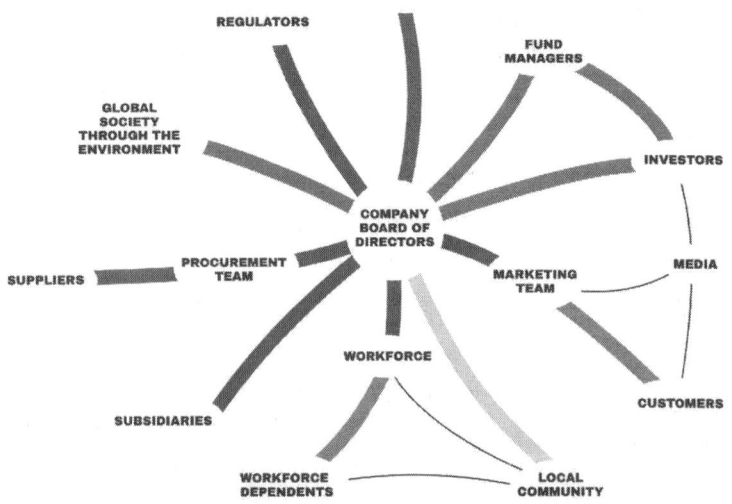

Main interest of stakeholder groups

- Company performance
- Short-term financial return
- Payment of interest and return of capital
- Regulatory compliance
- Environmental sustainability
- Price, payment, and long-term relationship
- Long-term community support and wellbeing
- Pay levels, work conditions, employment continuity
- Price and quality of products and service

The pursuit of growth by the company, with all the benefits this entails for many of its dependants, has become a quite different focus from the pursuit of profit by those who own its shares. When President Donald Trump spoke in the White House briefing room on 24 November 2020 to congratulate Americans on the Dow Jones Industrial Average breaking the "sacred number" of 30,000, he was taking an investor's view of economic success. Similar comments could have been made when the Dow Jones topped 380 for the first time in 1929, just prior to the Wall Street Crash, or 2,700 before Black Monday in 1987. While the population in general may benefit from economic growth, there is no simple equation to be drawn between stock indices and the wellbeing of all stakeholders around major companies. The volatility of price movement is intensified by the use of derivatives, synthetic deals, contracts for difference, spread betting, and the aggregation of shares in funds and funds of funds.

And hedge funds often short the market to profit from the price going down.

Thanks to the structure of listed companies and the financial markets that capitalise them, investors have often functioned like absentee landlords, with directors as their local factors, struggling to embrace in any meaningful way the global need to work together for social responsibility and sustainability, yet exerting constant pressure to provide short-term and ever-increasing financial return.

It is possible, of course, for individuals to be members of more than one stakeholder group. Some of those who strongly oppose global warming may have pension funds that depend on investments in net-carbon-emitting industries. Some of the investors benefitting from financial settlement following a buyout may be employees who are subsequently laid off by the new management.

In cultures where more emphasis is placed on the value of long-term mutuality, the rules of the company network may be different. Toyota Manufacturing UK is a European company with 260 parts and materials suppliers based in the UK and Europe, and suppliers of site services, many of which are in the local areas around Toyota's plants in Derbyshire and Flintshire, North Wales. Rules around competition between suppliers, which for many companies focus strongly on price, in Toyota's case aim at "developing mutually beneficial, long-term relationships based on mutual trust with all suppliers," pursuing "close and wide-ranging communication to share our business knowledge to enhance our business relationship."[28]

The much-emulated Toyota Production System involves alignment of stakeholders around the principal value of quality. Applying the doctrines of W. Edwards Deming, Toyota instilled the idea that everyone in the company was responsible for meeting the customer's expectations – an approach that underlay the company's reputation for reliability. That is, until new president Hiroshi Okuda challenged the company to increase its global market share from 7.3 per cent in 1995 to 10 per cent over the next decade, contributing in 2009 to the first of a series of highly publicised recalls of Toyota vehicles in the United States.[29]

Question 3: Is this arrangement fair?

How far does the network embody a balance of fairness for all parties, including future generations?

Not only do the stakeholders in a listed company tend to have different objectives, network rules can empower some stakeholders over others. Figure 5 examines fairness in a listed company network by indicating which relationships typically exert most influence over company decision-making.

Note that fairness, which concerns the distribution of power and resources in a network, is not the same as equality. Within a company, people can receive different amounts of remuneration, with different levels of risk attached, and work together in a chain of command that gives some individuals a degree of authority over others – all without anyone feeling the system is critically unfair. But fairness has a context, and that context is always evolving. If wages are frozen while directors award themselves generous share options, fairness will start to surface as an issue for employees. If a company increases the tariff on its customer care line while keeping telephone inquiries on hold, fairness will become an issue for its customer base.

Figure 5. Schematic model of stakeholder relationships in a listed company, suggesting through the thickness of the lines the interfaces most likely to influence company decision-making.

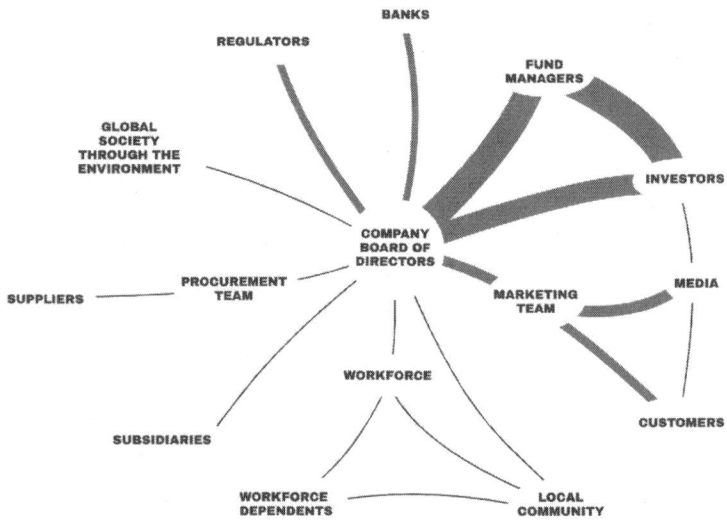

Historically, much of the discussion around fairness has focused on the relationship between management and investors.

In 1932, Adolf Berle and Gardiner Means documented the evolution of a new economic entity in America: the public corporation[30] – public because none of its numerous investors owned more than a small fraction of outstanding shares. These "dispersed shareholders", said Berle and Means, were rationally apathetic. They had little incentive to follow company affairs closely or even to vote. For their part, "corporate directors and professional executives, who usually worked for fixed fees and owned relatively little stock in the company, viewed themselves as stewards or trustees charged with guiding a vital social and economic institution in the interests of a wide range of beneficiaries. Certainly, they looked out for investors' interests, but they looked out for the interests of employees, customers, and the nation as well."[31]

This philosophy of "managerial capitalism" prevailed in the United States for roughly half a century, and had it continued to do so Figure 5 might have looked rather different. The period of relative economic stability in which managerial capitalism flourished, with good corporate financial results, came to an abrupt end, however, with President Nixon's decision to abandon the gold standard in 1971 (triggering inflation) and a significant increase in oil prices. The subsequent bear market saw the Dow Jones Industrial Average lose nearly half its value. Soon managerial capitalism fell into academic disrepute. A widely influential 1976 article by economist Michael Jensen and business school dean William Meckling titled "Theory of the Firm" argued that the "owners" of public corporations should be taking a more active interest in company affairs. The passivity of shareholders was, in their view, a serious weakness which led to directors neglecting shareholders' interests in favour of their own. Gradually a new business theory took shape under the banner of "shareholder primacy" in which the only legitimate purpose of the corporation was to maximise shareholder value.

In fact, contrary to popular belief, shareholders do not own the corporations in which they hold shares.[32] Nevertheless the doctrine of shareholder primacy found increasing support among a variety of interested parties. For journalists and academics, it offered a simple story about corporate structure and purpose. It proved personally profitable for activist corporate raiders in the 1980s and activist hedge funds in the 1990s and early 2000s. Top corporate executives could also benefit via an amendment of the US tax code in 1993 that tied executive pay to "objective" performance metrics. The obvious metric was the stock price – one that turned out to be easy to manipulate, at least in the short term. Through a combination of focus on share price and increasing shareholder influence over boards, shareholder primacy thus "led directly in the 1990s and 2000s to skyrocketing executive pay, increased earnings inequality, and more than a few spectacular accounting frauds."[33]

In the UK, shareholder primacy is enshrined in the Companies Act 2006, so that directors must act in the way they consider, in good faith, would be most likely to promote the success of the company for the benefit of its members, while having regard to certain stakeholder interests.[34] This reflects the principle of "enlightened shareholder value". Further, in the UK at least from as long ago as the Companies Act 1929, shareholders have been able to remove underperforming directors by resolution, whether or not this right is in the company's Articles.[35]

Recently, investors have been using their leverage to pursue the Environmental, Social and Governance (ESG) agenda. This reflects a significant change of sentiment. Note, however, that the underlying imbalance of fairness remains unresolved. The fact that influential fund managers currently champion an issue of public concern does not address the problem of investors holding disproportionate amounts of power. As long as, in the words of the American Business Roundtable, the interests of other stakeholders are relevant only "as a derivative of the duty to stockholders" fairness will almost inevitably remain an issue that, as John Maynard Keynes warned in 1933, is "likely or certain in the long run to set up strains and enmities which will bring to nought the financial calculation."[36] Jack Welch, former CEO of General Electric and formerly an advocate of shareholder primacy, put it rather more bluntly: "On the face of it, shareholder value is the dumbest idea in the world ... Shareholder value is a result, not a strategy ... Your main constituencies are your employees, your customers, and your products."[37]

By comparison with the influence of shareholders, the influence of employees on directors is relatively small, even though it includes obligations embedded in law (working hours, minimum wage) as well as commitments agreed in employment contracts. In 2016, Toshiba investors filed an action for compensatory damages of 300m yen (£1.6m) against former CEO Hisao Tanaka. Only passing attention was paid to the 14,000 workers who had lost their jobs as Toshiba downsized.[38]

Shareholder primacy also creates fairness issues for national governments, who may find themselves weighing the benefits of a tough taxation policy against the risk that a multinational will move its operation, and jobs, to a country with a lower tax regime. Amazon claimed in 2018 that "We pay all taxes required in the UK and every country where we operate." Nevertheless, critics point out that booking the company's sales through the UK branch of an overseas company, rather than through a UK-based subsidiary, means Amazon does not have to publish accounts detailing the tax it pays in respect of its total activities in the UK.[39] According to the *Times,* Amazon paid a total of £220 million in direct UK taxes in 2018, just over 2 per cent of its total revenues from doing business in the country (£10.9 billion).[40]

The G7 group of nations has recently stepped into this debate by proposing a global minimum corporation tax rate of 15 per cent, aimed at compelling companies to pay at least that rate of tax in the countries where they sell their products and services, and at eliminating tax rate competition between countries.[41] This was followed in October 2021 by 136 countries agreeing that the world's largest multinationals should pay a minimum of 15 per cent corporation tax, with tax being paid in countries where they operate and generate profits, regardless of whether they have a physical presence there.[42] The modest rate perhaps reflects the difficulty of achieving concerted action at a global level.

"We simply cannot take the capitalist system, which produces such plenty and so many solutions, for granted. Prosperity requires not just investment in economic capital, but investment in social capital. It is necessary to rebuild social capital to make markets work."

MARK CARNEY,
former Governor of the Bank of England, 2014.[43]

4. THE PATHOLOGY OF RELATIONAL INSTABILITY

In business networks, relational instability tends to produce five major symptoms that impact not only a company's performance and sustainability but also the surrounding social fabric. These are: the ready acceptance of debt as growth-accelerator; problems associated with excessive scale; extreme pay differentials; a powerful and often delayed regulatory response; and a shortening of planning timeframes.

Dependence on debt

Though normalised as a financial instrument for companies, nations and consumers, debt tends to be relationally destabilising.

In all contexts, borrower and lender have fundamentally different aims – the one to meet a short- or medium-term financial objective, the other to protect capital and gain interest. From the borrower's point of view, using debt finance involves a cost-benefit calculation – the benefit comprising, for example, the preservation of economic infrastructure during a pandemic or company expansion through acquisition or eventual home ownership, and the cost including interest on the loan and a risk to assets on which the loan may be secured. Usually, though, the lender is the stronger party, meaning that the relationship is asymmetrical and open to abuse. In a recent example, two major banks administering the UK government's coronavirus business interruption loans (CBIL), a key part of the government package to protect businesses during the Covid-19 pandemic, insisted the loans be secured on the personal property of the business owner, thus loading most of the default risk on the owner, not the bank. One candidate for the scheme was instead offered the bank's own product at 22 per cent interest (although this may have been exceptional). [44]

The most obvious reason for avoiding debt arrangements is that they increase susceptibility to shocks. Governments normally justify the public borrowing requirement on the grounds that, with sufficiently low interest rates relative to growth, revenues can be raised safely by increasing the debt to GDP ratio. But this leaves less room for manoeuvre should interest rates rise or growth be compromised. Interest rates have been at historic lows since the economic crisis of 2008 – itself triggered by debt defaults. In the decade that followed, most Western governments sought to protect public finances by reining in expenditure, raising political risk as voters respond to job losses and shrinking services by bolstering support for the Far Right and Far Left. The arrival of the pandemic has provoked a further heavy round of public borrowing and simultaneously caused growth to stall.

A similar susceptibility affects companies carrying heavy debt burdens. In companies, though, the decision to use debt finance may not reflect the interests of all stakeholders. Because limited liability makes shareholders relatively risk-tolerant, they will often allow or positively encourage directors to borrow heavily against company assets, using the financing to expand the business by acquisitions[45] or to fund dividend payments or share buybacks. According to a 2019 report by the OECD, global outstanding debt in the form of corporate bonds issued by non-financial companies had hit record levels by the end of 2018 – at US $13 trillion, double the equivalent figure for 2008. The OECD estimated that in the subsequent three years non-financial companies would have to "pay back or refinance about $4 trillion worth of corporate bonds, close to the total balance sheet of the US Federal Reserve."[46] The estimate, of course, was made pre-pandemic.

Perhaps the most problematic aspect of the relational instability of debt is the unfairness it creates for future generations. In a company, that might reflect the opportunity cost of diverting funds away from research and development or the loss of future jobs if insolvency forces the company into administration. At national level, future generations end up paying not just for genuine emergencies like a pandemic but for a long history of electorally-motivated tax cuts and fiscal mismanagement.

In September 2020, weighed down by Covid-19 spending, US national debt reached a new record of $3 trillion – the equivalent of an entire year's tax revenue.[47] Commenting on the prospects for US Millennials, *The Atlantic* paints a bleak picture: "They have smaller savings accounts than prior generations. They have less money invested. They own fewer houses to refinance or rent out or sell. They make less money, and are less likely to have benefits like paid sick leave. They have more than half a trillion dollars of student-loan debt to keep paying off, as well as hefty rent and child-care payments that keep coming due."[48]

Corporate giantism

Debt-funded acquisition allows companies to grow very large, very fast. According to Global Justice Now, corporations account for 157 of the 200 largest entities on the planet.[49] The world's largest company by revenue, US retail behemoth Wal-Mart, generated sales of $514 billion in 2018, more than the income of all but nine of the world's 195 national governments.[50]

Size doesn't have to exact a cost in human connectivity, but typically it does.

Internally, with longer chains of command, moving information and decision-approvals up and down the management line becomes time-consuming and inefficient. With no easy way to achieve consensus, corporate leadership feels remote and the planning process centralised and responsive mainly to data.

Customer loyalty schemes no longer involve human relationships but reduce themselves instead to financial inducements targeting specific subsets of the market. Organisation-wide pay structures, rules and procedures, though nominally fair, are apt to feel arbitrary and sometimes dehumanising.

Externally, corporate giants often have a Darwinian relationship with other businesses in the same sector, with conditions tending to reward size and market power (including scale efficiencies, access to cheaper sources of capital, and the ability to lower prices) rather than excellence and innovation. Not surprisingly, in the corporate playground bullying is common. The Global Restructuring Group of the Royal Bank of Scotland was accused of trying to "liquidate companies rather than support them" during the financial crisis.[51] It was estimated in 2019 that 50,000 small businesses fail every year because of cashflow problems created by late payment by their customers.[52]

In three ways, corporate giants also pose a challenge to government.

First, as noted earlier, size and geographical reach enable big companies to reduce tax liability, often by using transfer pricing between parent companies and their subsidiaries to book profits where tax rates are lowest. In the EU, because incorporation in any member state gives access to the entire single market, a corporation can domicile itself in a low-tax EU regime but still sell into the whole of the EU. According to a 2020 study, multinationals channelled €27 billion in profits generated in other countries through Ireland in 2016, suggesting that Ireland was the second-largest beneficiary of so-called profit shifting in the European Union, behind the Netherlands.[53]

Second, big companies sometimes control what amounts to essential infrastructure without being directly answerable to parliament. Google, for example, owns 90 per cent of the global search engine market outside China, giving it extensive influence over information flows. As such, companies can be a public liability without being publicly owned. "Too big to fail" means that some, notably in banking and insurance, are so central to the economy that in effect they enjoy privileged access to taxpayers' money. For example, Wall Street institutions benefited from a $700 billion facility in the Emergency Economic Stabilization Act (October 2008) authorising the government to purchase distressed assets.

Third, concentrating financial power into fewer, larger corporations distorts fairness in the political process. Even in mature democracies like those in Europe and North America, large corporations advance their interests through political lobbying in subtle and creative ways. This rarely involves calling in personal favours from journalists or MPs. The new tactics include recruiting teams of sympathetic experts to promote a particular position, forging online reviews, funding sympathetic thinktanks, flooding the web with positive information, and removing critical mentions from Wikipedia.[54]

Traditionally, part of this battle for influence has involved buying up news media outlets – Amazon, for example, now owning the *Washington Post*. More significantly, though, *a few corporate giants are redefining human connectivity at the global scale by writing interaction rules into social media platforms and by tying advertising revenue to clickable content.*

A notable recent example is Twitter's role in shaping political discourse in the 2020 US Presidential election. More widely, big IT corporates struggle to moderate content, with Facebook CEO Mark Zuckerberg admitting that, with 2.7 billion users and tens of billions of posts shared every day, "at our scale we'll always make mistakes and decisions that people disagree with."[55] Both Facebook and Instagram have been at the centre of public controversies over their failure to delete harmful online content – one of a number of issues over which they have been in confrontation with European regulators.[56]

Extreme pay differentials

Weakening of mutual knowledge in a large organisation doesn't on its own result in disengagement. For example, a study of 17,498 male and 17,897 female employees from thirty EU countries sampled in the sixth European Working Conditions Survey (2015) found "no association between work engagement and the size of the company".[57] There is, though, a strong link with fairness. While most employees would not begrudge generous remuneration to a hard-working top executive, excessive and apparently unjustified pay differentials are divisive both socially and politically.

In 2021, it took the average FTSE-100 CEO just 34 hours at work to pass median earnings.[58] According to

CBS News, in the US "CEO compensation rose 940 per cent from 1978 to 2018, compared with a 12 per cent rise in pay for the average American worker during the same period."[59] Among the 350 largest US companies, average CEO pay in 2018 was $17.2 million. The average ratio between the US chief executive's pay and that of the median worker was 287:1 in 2018, up from 58:1 in 1989 and 20:1 in 1965.[60] In the same period, Warren Buffett's company Berkshire Hathaway Inc. had the lowest pay ratio of all S&P 500 companies: just 2:1 – though the fact that Buffett owns roughly $100 billion of Berkshire stock effectively makes this an outlier.[61]

Increasingly, as noted earlier, the issue of executive pay has come into the sights of activists and other investors. On 6 May 2021, the *Financial Times* reported that more than 60 per cent of shareholders at Anglo-Australian miner Rio Tinto's AGM opposed a remuneration report recognising former chief executive Jean-Sébastien Jacques' 20 per cent pay increase and share options worth £27 million. At the centre of the dispute was the relationship with local community stakeholders, Rio Tinto having made the decision to blast the 46,000-year-old Juukan Gorge site in Western Australia to make way for a mine expansion. Among those voting against the report were Norway's $1.3 trillion oil fund and the UK's Local Authority Pension Fund Forum.[62]

Heavy regulation

Because multinationals transcend different regulatory regimes, big-scale business tends to encourage big-scale government and the transfer of power to transnational bodies more remote from the individual citizens whose interests are, at least in theory, being protected.[63]

According to a list compiled by investment bank Keefe, Bruyette and Woods, US banks have been fined a total of $243 billion since the 2008 financial crisis, mainly for misleading investors about the quality of mortgages packaged into bonds. Not all the fines were paid in cash, with Goldman Sachs committing to pay $1.8 billion in the form of loan forgiveness and financing for affordable housing.[64] In 2018, Google was fined €4.3 billion ($4.8 billion) by EU regulators for imposing illegal restrictions on Android device manufacturers — the culmination of a three-year investigation, and adding to the €2.4 billion fine imposed the previous year for hampering rivals of shopping comparison websites.[65]

Big regulation, though, doesn't guarantee compliance. Partly this is because companies innovate faster than governments can legislate, meaning that regulation, even by the strongest authorities, lags behind the changes it seeks to oversee. When high-frequency trading (HFT) was implicated in severe market crashes in 2010 and 2013, the European Parliament did not enact legislation until April 2014, with a further delay until January 2017 to allow member states to implement the new rules. There is also a cost to increasing the legal and regulatory burden. It is no coincidence that the most recent primary company law passed in the UK, the Companies Act 2006, runs to 1,300 sections (before schedules) and is the longest ever UK statute, potentially discriminating against businesses that cannot afford lawyers to cut through red tape (including startups, small and medium size companies) and putting innovation at risk.

Overall, an extensive study of corporate scandals and regulations across 26 countries spanning the years 1800 to 2015 found "no evidence that regulations can effectively curb future corporate misconduct. Rather, today's regulations are a strong predictor of future fraudulent behaviour because firms are quick to adapt to the new rules and move their activities to unregulated areas; because regulators rely on explicitly laid-out rules to be able to identify and prosecute corporate wrongdoing; or because the new regulations have unintended consequences."[66]

Obsession with the short term

Based on a survey of more than 1,000 C-suite executives and board members reporting in late 2015 and early 2016, the McKinsey Global Institute concluded that "A majority of respondents said that the pressure to generate strong financial results within two years was growing. In the two years since a similar survey was conducted, the share of respondents who reported such pressure rose from 79 per cent to 87 per cent."[67]

Inevitably, short-termism pulls emphasis away from other priorities. Direct intervention by activist funds, who buy shares with a view to gaining seats on the board and unlocking short-term value for shareholders, results in fewer strategic operational or growth objectives and typically can leave hollowed-out companies with little resilience to economic downturns. Companies with a short-term perspective are likely to invest less in capital equipment and research and development than firms with longer-term horizons.[68] If, in a few years' time, antibiotics are no longer able to provide a cure for pneumonia, it will in part be because pharmaceutical companies have been reluctant to commit funding to research that could take two decades to bring a low-priced product to market.[69]

By contrast, McKinsey's research shows that, compared to others, US companies focusing on the long term achieved 47 per cent greater average revenue and 36 per cent higher earnings growth – not to mention superior total return to shareholders. "The returns to society and the overall economy were equally impressive. By our measures, companies that were managed for the long term added nearly 12,000 more jobs on average than their peers from 2001 to 2015. We calculate that US GDP over the past decade might well have grown by an additional $1 trillion if the whole economy had performed at the level of our sample of companies that make the cut as long-term, generating some five million additional jobs over this period."[70]

An underlying problem with short-termism revolves around tenure. Shareholders and directors are both fairly ephemeral figures in a corporation. Globally, CEOs stay in post for an average of five years.[71] They are apt to trim their objectives accordingly. A top executive in his or her late fifties may be setting up for retirement. Investors move on if tough trading conditions force a company to cut its dividend. It is other stakeholders, more strongly tied to the company's fortunes, who will be left with the risk of loss when things go wrong – particularly suppliers, local communities and employees.

5. HOW A COMPANY CAN TACKLE RELATIONAL INSTABILITY

It is not a new thought to emphasise relationships in business. As John Browne (former CEO of BP) wrote in 2015: "The logic is simple and compelling. The success of a company depends on its relationships with the external world, not just customers and investors, but also employees, regulators, politicians, activists, NGOs, the environment and technology. Choices made through the business, from the boardroom to the shop floor, affect that relationship. For the company to be successful, decision-taking in every division and at every level must take account of these effects."[72]

This is especially important in periods of political, social and financial turbulence. The global economy and financial system in 2022 is still in the cloud of the pandemic. Although supply chains may be back to normal later in the year, the effects on levels of employment, and use of the internet for meetings so as to avoid local and international travel, are probably here to stay. In addition, competition for global influence between US and China, and resulting political instability in many parts of the world due to proxy wars, are likely to continue to impact corporate supply chains and patterns of demand. In such a context, companies' relationships with their stakeholders are crucial for their financial stability and sustainability.

The idea of relational instability allows us to assess the strength of those relationships and to treat them as an infrastructural asset – not just at a personal level but across a company's entire stakeholder network.

More than that, the idea of relational instability provides boards of directors with a clear rationale for addressing recent and widely-discussed concerns about the impact of business on society and the environment.

In what might be termed a *relational company*, two operational ideas are front and centre.

First and foremost, company boards should take account of all the major stakeholder interests and not give priority to any one of them.

As indicated earlier, the idea that the powers and benefits bestowed by incorporation are *a privilege that carries a degree of public responsibility* has never quite vanished from view, and has moved more centre-stage with a slew of legal requirements and general recommendations that a company should address, and report on, as to the impact it makes on employee wellbeing, local communities and the environment amongst other things.

But in the end, it isn't enough to broadcast ESG-compliant messaging to the world at large if the company retains what is, in all but name, a shareholder-centric model of corporate governance. The relational company model embeds parity of stakeholder interests simply by requiring fairness across the networks over which the company has influence. But it also urges that a company board works *with major shareholders* to reposition the company's constitution towards a broader stakeholder-centric model – a move that under UK law does not require any legislative change.[73] That single move – the first of ten principles covered in this chapter – is a foundational declaration of purpose.

Suggested wording for that purpose in a company constitution is given in the next section. In practice it means that the board will consider other stakeholders not merely as instruments to serve the interests of shareholders but as having intrinsic value in themselves for decision-making in the best interests of the company over time. The board recognises and values the contribution of all the main stakeholders to the success of the business and puts their interests at the heart of company decision-making and operations.

It is up to the board, working on a case-by-case basis and as circumstances require, to determine whether the long-term interests of particular stakeholder groups need to be balanced, prioritised or traded off – the key phrase here being "long term", since returning short-term profit to shareholders may not be for the long-term benefit and sustainability of the company.

It is recognised that such decisions will always involve the exercise of judgment by the directors. It is also recognised that most boards will find themselves operating within tight parameters in going against shareholder interests. Investors are a significant stakeholder group, and relatively mobile compared to other groups whose long-term fortunes can be much more closely tied to those of the company.

Difficult questions would arise for directors when the interests of one of these stakeholder groups comes into direct conflict with the interests of investors, on whose continued support the company depends, and of whom a portion may choose to sell up and move on if, for example, the board decides to reduce the dividend. This might arise if the directors wish to make a generous pay increase for employees or decide to make a substantial contribution to clear the pension fund deficit.

The South African Corporate Governance Code faces up to this by saying that because what is in the best interests of the company is not necessarily always equated to the best interests of shareholders, they do not necessarily have a predetermined precedence over other stakeholders. The wording suggested for the purpose of the company in the next section does not specifically address this issue but leaves it for the directors to decide how to interpret what is in the best interests of the company. It is interesting to note that the American Business Roundtable's declaration – "We commit to deliver value to all of [our stakeholders], for the future success of our companies, our communities and our country" – stops short of advising on how potential conflicts of interest might be handled.[74]

Second, the company should seek to increase efficiency and productivity by treating improved internal and external relationships as a means to add value.

The other nine principles in the chapter are, in the main, about the way in which business itself is carried out, and refer to different ways of building human connectivity across a variety of stakeholder groups in the company network.

There is plenty of evidence that an approach treating relationships as an asset has positive outcomes for companies. A report published in 2020 by investment manager BlackRock, for example, indicated that companies with stronger social scores, which in part provide a proxy measure of human connectivity in companies (better customer relations, better workforce management) did better in the coronavirus lockdown.[75]

For several years, the polling group Gallup has pioneered research behind employee engagement in a series of groundbreaking studies. "The findings consistently show that the relationship between each element of engagement and performance at the workgroup level is sustainable and highly generalisable across organisations."[76] Gallup's diagnostic 12-question survey measures aspects of human connectivity from the perspective of employees within a company. Where employees are "psychological owners," this drives high performance and innovation and moves the organisation forward in terms of productivity, profitability, and employee retention and turnover. Comparing the most engaged teams with the least engaged, Gallup suggest that the former show 41 per cent lower absenteeism,

10 per cent higher customer metrics, and 21 per cent higher profitability.

A pioneer in building human connectivity in relations with suppliers is the Japanese car manufacturer Toyota. Like many global companies, Toyota relies on vast and complex supply lines delivering thousands of parts for its eighty or so different models on a "just-in-time" basis that avoids expensive stockpiling. The Toyota Production System (TPS) is a set of principles, most of which govern the way different stakeholders within the company's ecosystem interact. Notably, while being challenged to meet the highest standards, suppliers are treated as part of the company's "extended family" and are "not kicked out except for the most egregious behavior".[77] At the point where Toyota's ideas on lean manufacturing were gaining traction with manufacturers worldwide, *Industry Week* reported large auto-parts manufacturer Freudenberg-NOK as crediting TPS with "reducing its defect rate by more than 2,000 parts per million to less than 50, cutting quality costs by 60 per cent, slashing work-in-process inventory by 80 per cent, and improving labor productivity by 25 per cent annually."[78]

Figure 6. The model for creating a relational company.

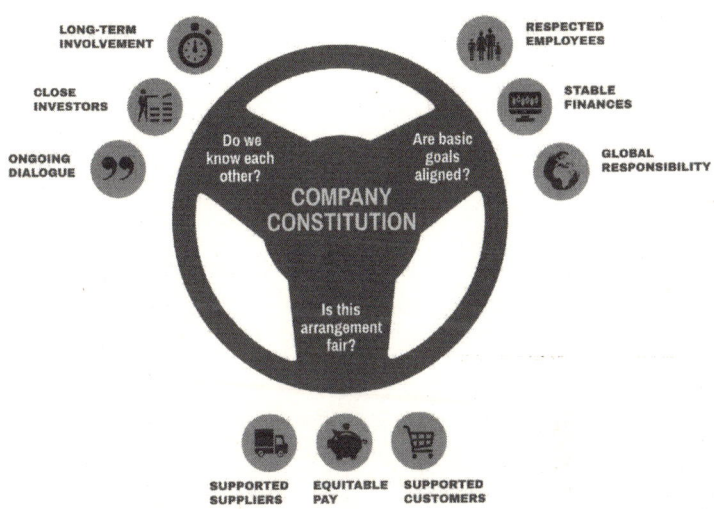

Figure 6 gives a visual representation of the relational company model. The ten principles (including the first, revision of the company constitution) fall into three groups that correspond to the three questions around which this book is based. They are not the only initiatives that could be taken, but they are highlighted here, and form the basis of a Relational Stability Strategy for Business, for three main reasons:

- First, with the exception of changing the company constitution, which requires shareholder approval, they can be actioned directly by a company's board.
- Second, because they are relatively transparent to outsiders using publicly available sources of information.
- And third, because they provide a basis for metrics by which progress in tackling relational instability can

be measured (for further information on metrics, see Appendix 1).

In the rest of this chapter, each principle of the Strategy is broken down into specific action points, with examples of companies – many of them major global corporates – at least a part of whose operation already works by strengthening human connectivity through following the principles set out in the Strategy.

Relational Stability Strategy for Business

1. Redefine the purpose of the company and make it known to investors, directors and employees

Suggested wording for the purpose of the company is as follows:

> *The purpose of the company is to serve society through long-term value creation in the interests of all its major stakeholders, in particular employees, suppliers, customers and shareholders, while honouring wider responsibilities to local communities and the environment.*
>
> *Recognising that human connectivity based on mutual knowledge, alignment of interests and fairness is key to achieving a sustainable and successful business, the directors will ensure there is regular measurement of the quality of key relationships leading to dialogue with all the main stakeholders, and will oversee and manage the company for their long-term benefit.*

This embeds an ethos of relational stability at the heart of company management and operations, the goal being to formalise the company's focus on relationships between its stakeholders and to bring this to the attention of all levels of management from the board down. Directors of companies will need to evaluate the impact of their decisions and actions on all major stakeholder groups.

Key recommendations:

- **Create a post of Stakeholder Relationships Director**. This sends a clear message to the corporate world and society in general that the company intends to persevere in, and give priority to, a stakeholder-inclusive approach. A Stakeholder Relationships Director is a full-time executive with similar status at board level to the directors of finance and HR, and tasked with managing communication and liaison with the company's core stakeholders, and with third parties such as trades unions and trade associations. The scope of the role would be worked out alongside the responsibilities of the other directors.
- **Invest in the company's media to emphasise the change of stance.** Mission statement, website, company reports, social media and advertising should consistently reinforce the values the company stands for. Training – for staff, management, business partners and fund management investors – will help to embed company ethos and explore its implications for key operational areas. Fund management investors, for example, will need to

know that the company is seeking "patient capital" that allows financial returns to be made over a longer timeframe.

Companies already engaging with this

AmerisourceBergen. The $136 billion American drug wholesale company in the past described its mission as "To build shareholder value by delivering pharmaceutical and healthcare products, services and solutions in innovative and cost-effective ways. We will realise this mission by setting the highest standards in service, reliability, safety and cost containment in our industry." The company has now altered its mission statement to read: "We understand that our duty as a company extends beyond the services we provide, the customers we serve, the team members we employ, and the communities where we live and work. It means we understand our moral obligation to improve the wellbeing of human and animal populations by expanding access to quality healthcare, operating sustainably, and upholding the highest standards of safety and quality ..."[79]

Unilever. The consumer goods company states that its organisational purpose is "to add vitality to life. We meet everyday needs for nutrition, hygiene and personal care with brands that help people feel good, look good and get more out of life." Note that nowhere is the term "maximising shareholder value" referenced as part of its purpose. Instead, this $56 billion market value company inspires a higher sense of meaning for its 155,000 employees worldwide and the millions of customers that use its products each day – all the while determined to leave the world a better place.[80]

Casio. According to its mission statement, the Japanese electronics giant is committed "to contributing to society by offering the kind of original, useful products that only Casio can. Products with innovative functions assist people in their daily lives and keep society moving forward."[81]

2. Promote dialogue among all significant stakeholder groups, using live meetings and digital platforms

Interaction has a number of benefits – particularly when it occurs between groups that rarely come in contact with one another.

Structures and procedures that enable meaningful discussion between levels of seniority in a company, and between the workforce and investors, are likely to help labour relations and reassure employees that shareholders are not simply "absentee landlords". As indicated earlier, employees whose views are listened to and whose interests are represented at board level will be more engaged and productive and less likely to resign, take time off for sickness, or join strike action. Also, as pointed out in the Harvard Business Review, "By taking an active part to the life of the company, workers and management can engage in win-win negotiations at times of economic difficulties as workers are more aware of the constraints a company is facing and the rationale behind the choices made."[82]

Key recommendations:

- **Hold quarterly meetings (one of which would be the AGM) as opportunities to engage the full breadth of stakeholder membership.** Regularly invite shareholders and employees, and at least once a year extend this invitation to other major stakeholders (customers, suppliers, banks, creditors, customers, civic leaders, representatives of the local community), accepting that the need for confidentiality may require some groups to attend different meetings. Enable geographically distant stakeholders to participate live online.
- **Hold quarterly meetings in different locations,** depending on where the company's operations are situated and where shareholders are resident. If the company (or group of companies) operates in a number of countries, quarterly meetings can be held in each country where the group is active. Encourage attendance by holding meetings at different times, including evenings and weekends.
- **Extend the business of the meeting to include social and educational content** which will deepen stakeholders' knowledge both of the company's plans and operations and of each other. Also provide for break-out meetings that allow employees and other stakeholders access to company officials, for instance the finance director, whose work may be little understood.
- **Be present in the public space.** Use a full repertoire of communication media – Twitter, Facebook, Instagram, newsletters, reports, presentations,

speeches, videos, podcasts, interviews, training, entertainment events, town hall meetings, open houses, tours, ratings, performance metrics – to make the company visible to its stakeholders, subject always to rules on reporting of confidential and price-sensitive information.

- **Invite feedback**. Use surveys, focus groups, assessments, public hearings, workshops, online feedback or discussion forums and hotlines to facilitate a flow of information to the company, and encourage two-way or multi-party conversation (advisory boards, task forces, leadership summits, interviews, research and analysis, workshops, focus groups) in which stakeholders can play an important advisory role in decision-making.

- **Use integrated reporting** to formalise the company's accountability not just for its financial results and returns but also for its impact on non-financial capital (human, natural, manufactured, intellectual) and the steps it has taken to consider, promote and protect the interests of other stakeholders.[83]

- **Leverage the creativity of the workforce** by putting in place procedures to discuss ideas from all employees and to recognise and reward innovation.

- **Value the role of bridging individuals.** Recognise and build on the abilities of people who belong to more than one stakeholder group and are therefore in a unique position to bring differing interests together.

Companies already engaging with this

BAE Systems. The leading international defence, security and aerospace company, headquartered in London and with a total workforce of more than 85,800, has over a number of years used structured forums and open discussions to build a relationship of trust with its UK trade unions. The company has high levels of union membership, and pays for full-time union conveners on each of its sites.[84] Separately, the company has a bargaining and consultation framework at group level. BAE systems has not faced industrial action in the UK in the last 15 years.[85]

Hyundai. The global automobile manufacturer holds conference calls at different times of day to cater for investors around the world.[86]

L'Oréal. Headquartered in Paris, L'Oréal is the world's largest cosmetics and beauty products company, with sales in 2020 of €29.8 billion. It has 88,000 employees worldwide and a stated aim of being exemplary in its business ethics.[87] Each October the company holds an ethics day at which the entire workforce is invited to put questions directly to the Chairman and Chief Executive, Jean-Paul Agon. In 2018 it had a network of 75 ethics correspondents throughout the business.[88] L'Oréal's approach to ethics goes beyond compliance with rules. The company aims to engage its large international staff and to help them make good decisions in situations where issues are not clear-cut. Its four ethical principles are integrity (discouraging lying and cheating), respect (treating others as they would wish to be treated), courage (speaking up in ethically difficult situations) and transparency (promoting an open environment in which there is less need for formal procedures and controls). The company also operates a no-blame policy – *le droit de l'erreur* (the right to make mistakes). Its standard procedure is to understand the mistake, to introduce corrective measures, and to encourage the employee to tell the story for the benefit of colleagues.

Coca-Cola. Although by the year 2000 Coca-Cola had, for its own workers, the best policies in Africa for AIDS prevention, protection, testing and treatment, protesters demanded that the company should provide the same services to its bottling affiliates. As the affiliates were completely separate entities, Coca-Cola at first resisted the move on costs grounds. But with global activists raising the issue at AIDS conferences, the board decided to act. They found bridging leaders from all sides of the debate, and provided an opportunity for antagonists to meet in an environment that stressed their role as human beings caring deeply about the same outcomes. Ultimately, Coca-Cola provided AIDS services for bottling affiliates' employees throughout Africa with each stakeholder group – including the affiliates and employees – paying some costs.[89]

McDonald's. In 2017, shareholder activists pushed the global fast-food chain to assess the environmental damage caused by using foam containers. Although a shareholder resolution aimed at ending foam container usage received only 32 per cent of votes at the AGM, the company nevertheless decided to cease using plastic foam cups in 2018 and created a plan to use recycled sources for all fibre-based packaging by 2020.[90] In fact the company fell short of the target (as of 2020, McDonald's reports, "78 per cent of our global guest packaging weight comes from fiber materials"[91]), but other providers in the competitive fast-food market had already followed suit.

Hitachi. For the past ten years, alongside quarterly meetings and AGMs, the Japanese multinational has organised an "Integrated Reporting day". The agenda includes remarks from the CEO and updates on the different industry sectors the company is involved in (including energy, industry, IT, and mobility). Hitachi is also heavily invested in social media, with a large archive of company-related information and regular updates on YouTube, LinkedIn, Facebook and Twitter, where followers number in the hundreds of thousands.[92]

KEPCO. The Korean Electric Power Corporation has an online form allowing any member of the public to voice their opinion on the company's sustainability management from the viewpoint of their own particular stakeholder interest.[93]

Fujifilm. One of the world's largest photography and imaging companies, Fujifilm uses integrated reporting directly on its corporate website. Its annual report also lays out the company's strategy for economic and social value creation.[94]

Yamaha. In 2018, following the Paris Agreement on climate change, Yamaha Motor Corporation's President and CEO Yoshihiro Hidaka committed the company to "solving societal issues and achieving continuous growth by creating *Kando* in a way unique to Yamaha." *Kando* is a Japanese word referencing the feeling of deep satisfaction and intense excitement a person experiences when encountering something of exceptional value. "Going forward," he said, "we will engage in a commitment to international agreements, while emphasising harmony with local communities, society at large and the global environment, and promote activities that will lead to the realisation of a sustainable society, to become a company that earns the trust of stakeholders."[95]

Shutterstock. For two days each summer, most of Shutterstock's staff put regular work on hold and come up with new, creative ideas that can be executed in just 24 hours. This Shutterstock Hackathon has been growing bigger (and more competitive) every year since 2011. The rules are simple: "You have 24 hours to build something awesome." To be eligible for prizes, teams have to include members from at least three different departments, and are encouraged to collaborate with people they would otherwise never work with. The 400 employees, in 52 teams, comprise 60 per cent of Shutterstock's workforce.[96]

3. Work towards having a significant proportion of the shares owned by employees, individuals or family trusts

Indirect ownership of shares – through managed funds and nominee accounts – can be partially offset by having brokers direct the shares of a selling institution towards individual investors and family trusts. Similarly, the principal-agent problem of workforce motivation is diminished where share schemes help to build ownership of shares by employees, giving them a greater interest in, and commitment to, the company and its business. If the company operates from one principal geographic location, there are also benefits in encouraging local ownership of shares, as shareholders living in the same city or region are likely to have a long-term interest in the company's profitability and local employment, and may themselves be a source of technical expertise or marketing connections.

BlackRock, one of the largest investment institutions, has announced that it will grant its larger investment clients (such as pension funds) the power to vote on matters in companies in which they indirectly hold shares through the fund manager. This should encourage the capital providers to take an interest in and responsibility for operations of the companies in which they indirectly invest.[97] However, the capital providers who have the ultimate interest in the shares (and the wellbeing of the company) may not be given any right to vote as the investment may be held through a number of invested funds.[98]

Companies already engaging with this

The Technology Partnership (TTP). Originally established in the 1970s, TTP Group is a range of businesses focused on meeting the needs of companies planning to flourish through the use of technology and innovation. Responding to the call of the UK government in 2020, the TTP team worked around the clock to develop CoVent – a fully functioning mass-manufacturable ventilator – achieving in weeks something that would normally take years. According to its 2020 Annual Report, nearly all of the Group's 892 shareholders are employees or ex-employees, including children, spouses/civil partners and family trusts. Shareholders are among a range of stakeholder groups whose needs are examined and monitored through the report. "The directors seek to consider the long-term consequences of any decision and the impact on the staff and other key stakeholders."[99]

Marks and Spencer. When retailer Sir Philip Green made a bid for Marks and Spencer in 2004, he was supported by roughly a third of the company's institutional shareholders. The attempt failed, mainly thanks to the loyalty of small shareholders who attended the annual general meeting in force. In 2017, the company set up a private shareholder panel and gave members access to the board. They received over 1,200 applications, from which they randomly selected five, commenting that private shareholders "are not only financially invested in M&S; they are some of our most loyal customers who care deeply about our business.

Our future success is dependent on our ability to adapt to our customers' changing needs and to deliver this we need to engage with a wide range of stakeholders, including our private shareholders."[100]

VINCI. The French integrated concessions-construction company encourages employees to become shareholders. In 2018, over half of the company's workforce (130,000 people) owned shares through different schemes, with 90 per cent of the Group's employees eligible for an employee saving scheme in 31 countries. By the end of the same year, the VINCI employee shareholder club, set up in 2011, had around 14,000 members. Altogether, the Group's employees own almost 9 per cent of its share capital.[101]

Huawei. Though questions have been raised about its susceptibility to political influence, the Chinese telecoms giant is privately held and employee-owned. According to the BBC, this gave it the power to invest more money into research and development. Each year, Huawei spends US$20 billion on research and development – one of the biggest research budgets in the world. By contrast, says founder and chairman Ren Zhengfei, "Publicly listed companies have to pay a lot of attention to their balance sheets. They can't invest too much, otherwise profits will drop and so will their share prices. At Huawei, we fight for our ideals. We know that if we fertilise our 'soil' it will become more bountiful. That's how we've managed to pull ahead and succeed."[102]

Symology. The UK company develops and supplies integrated solutions for the management of infrastructure assets, including highways, land and property, bridges and structures, public lighting, and distribution networks. Being employee-owned has shielded the firm from pressures to deliver short-term profitability. Instead, it allocates resources towards research and development – developing cutting-edge asset management systems. This long-term orientation in turn has ensured deep client relationships.[103]

Bouygues. The large French conglomerate led by Martin Bouygues, a second-generation family member, has 20.3 per cent of its share capital owned by employees, giving them 27.4 per cent of voting rights. Since its introduction in 1970, the development of employee share ownership at Bouygues has remained a priority for the Group, placing it at the top of the CAC 40 rankings for employee share ownership.[104]

4. Work towards having a high proportion of shares owned on a long-term basis

In a financial environment focused on immediate returns, there is a strong case for companies incentivising long-term share ownership – whether the company is listed or private. Companies, of course, cannot dictate investor behaviour. But they can offer incentives that encourage investors to remain invested. Patrick Bolton of Columbia Business School has advocated so-called "loyalty shares" whose voting rights increase the longer they are held by the investor.[105]

Ideas of this kind are already beginning to find their way into custom and practice in some countries. Former Chief Economist of the Bank of England Andrew Haldane has noted a number of initiatives, including France's introduction of a so-called *Florange* law in 2014, "automatically granting shareholders in French-listed companies double voting rights if they are held for two years or longer. A similar law has recently passed in Italy, with loyalty shares automatically granted provided there is approval by two-thirds of shareholders. The provision for enhanced voting rights for longer-term shareholders has also been discussed in the context of the EU Shareholder Rights Directive."[106]

Key recommendation:

- **Reward long-term share ownership**. Shareholders agree by resolution that additional shares be issued to those who have held their shares for a minimum of three years. Additional financial incentives might include increasing the amount of the dividend on their shares. Longer-term shareholders (individual or managers of funds) could also be accorded special recognition, exclusive discounts on company products, invitations to prestigious events, or the right to appoint a non-executive director to the board who, in addition to normal duties, would be tasked with reporting to, and discussing issues with, this particular interest group. Shareholders who are individuals or family trusts would gain these benefits directly. In respect of shares held in managed or other funds, the benefits could accrue to the fund which should benefit their capital providers, so far as financial rewards are concerned, and to the fund managers so far as other benefits are concerned. Consideration could be given to splitting funds so that capital providers can invest in managed funds which in turn invest in companies on a long-term basis.

Companies already engaging with this

Air Liquide. Air Liquide, a French multinational with 67,000 employees in 80 countries, which provides gas, technology and services for industry and health, was created in 1902 by a small group of direct shareholders. These remain a differentiating feature of the company. At the end of 2019, 420,000 individual shareholders held some 32 per cent of company share capital.[107] Air Liquide believes in promoting and encouraging long-term share ownership, through transparent investor relations, strong mutual respect, regular dividend growth, and loyalty bonuses for long-term shareholders. All investors, individual and institutional, who have held registered shares (either direct or through an intermediary) for more than two full calendar years, can benefit from a loyalty bonus comprising a 10 per cent dividend increase and a 10 per cent allocation of free additional stock. Shares must be held until dividend payment and free share attribution dates (generally in May–June). Floated on the Paris Stock Exchange in 1913, the company paid its first dividends in 1907 and has continued to do so. The payout ratio has been stable for the last ten years at around 50 per cent of the group net profit. Over the last 30 years, dividends have been increased regularly or at least maintained.[108]

The Long-Term Stock Exchange (LTSE). Brainchild of American writer and blogger Eric Ries, who proposed the idea in his 2011 book *The Lean Startup*, the LTSE was launched to enable new companies to raise capital while keeping their focus on long-term rather than short-term results. LTSE is registered with the US Securities and Exchange Commission (SEC) with listing standards that, according to President Emeritus Michelle Greene, "are designed to create a new public market experience that aligns modern companies and investors focused on creating value over generations."[109] The new exchange imposes additional rules on listed companies and their investors, besides the rules required by law and traditional exchanges. Because these additional rules are imposed by an exchange, they can be enforced by existing mechanisms at the SEC. On 26 August 2021, Asana Inc. and Twilio Inc. became the first two companies to be listed on the LTSE.

5. Ensure that management has respect for the interests of employees

Companies have significant influence over the lives of their employees. The wellbeing of employees' families is affected strongly by company pay policy, redundancy programmes and company failure. Shorter working hours translate into more time for employees to recharge with their families and friends, and to engage in sport and other activities. However, the attempt to offload cost and risk by engaging staff on zero-hours contracts has created a new environment where employees have more flexibility but also more uncertainty and, often, lower pay.

Globally, a study published by the World Health Organization (WHO) in 2021 showed that in 2016 745,000 people died from stroke and heart disease due to working long hours, with people living in South East Asia and the Western Pacific region most affected. The research indicated that a work week exceeding 55 hours raised the risk of stroke by 35 per cent and the risk of heart disease by 17 per cent, compared to a working week of 35–40 hours.[110]

The benefits of the gig economy to employers are often illusory: research in the UK shows that a portfolio of firms with high employee satisfaction outperforms its peers by 2.3 to 3.8 per cent per annum or a cumulative 89 to 184 per cent over 28 years.[111] Encouraging, incentivising and listening to employees leads to greater loyalty and productivity, with lower numbers of employees leaving and less absence through illness or stress.

It should also be noted that the link between working hours and productivity is not linear. Trials of a four-day working week in Iceland, in which workers were paid the same amount for shorter hours, were recently hailed as an "overwhelming success". The trials, which took place between 2015 and 2019, included more than 2,500 workers in preschools, offices, social service providers, and hospitals. Productivity remained the same or improved in the majority of workplaces, researchers said.[112]

Key recommendations:

- **Encourage employees to take their full holiday entitlement**, and make that entitlement generous enough to allow a genuine break to be with family and friends. Also, make it clear that employees are not expected to communicate with their office during vacations, or to add two hours to their working day by responding to emails from home. Ensure that employees take at least one full day off each weekend.
- **Look after employees' physical and emotional health.** Offer flexibility over hours and home-working around maternity/paternity leave and family crises. Make available guidance for personal issues such as stress at work, illness, marriage problems and childcare. Provide free regular health checks. Provide sabbaticals of one to three months on full pay for all staff when they have worked uninterrupted for a seven-year period for the company.
- **Have a robust approach to sexual harassment and bullying in the workplace**. Actively enforce a zero-tolerance policy on harassment and bullying, and ensure that complaints are taken seriously and appropriate action taken. Also have in place policies protecting employees from illegal discrimination on grounds of age, gender, disability, and sexual orientation.
- **Encourage employees at all levels of seniority to mix,** for instance at company social events and through activities such as an office choir, broadening the range of connections and building shared experience outside the processes of the workplace.

- **Enable employees to locate closer to relatives** so that they can better look after dependent family members (particularly children and the elderly). This proposal applies mainly to larger companies which have stores, services or manufacturing facilities in a number of different parts of the country (see the example from John Lewis below).
- **Provide generous pay with productivity bonuses and share incentive schemes** for all employees. Do not have zero-hours contracts of the type which provide for pay only when work is requested, if the employee is prohibited from working elsewhere.
- **Where possible, institute a work-from-home policy**. For instance, a balance of three days home, two days office, per week. This would give people the advantages of the office networks, while giving them more time to spend with families by cutting out time-expensive commutes. The pandemic lockdown has shown the potential of this.

Companies already engaging with this

Quorum Network Resources Ltd. This IT services company is one of several to have signed up to The Scottish Business Pledge – a values-led partnership between government and business which embodies "a shared ambition of boosting productivity, competitiveness, sustainable employment, and workforce engagement and development." Quorum, says Andrew Watson, Co-Founder and Managing Director, is "standing proof that you can treat your employees, customers, and suppliers with equal respect and pay people a decent salary for a fair day's work and still make a profit at the end of the year." The company regards the wellbeing of employees' families as its direct responsibility. "The work we do with Family Friendly Working Scotland is based on the idea that when you employ one person, you also enter into a contract with their whole family and I believe we should always be aware that our actions as Business Leaders and employers have implications beyond the simple employee/employer contract. We have a responsibility for the wellbeing of the family unit as well."[113]

The John Lewis Partnership. John Lewis has a distinctive corporate structure that was designed by founder John Spedan Lewis to be both commercially competitive and democratic. All permanent staff are Partners who through a trust arrangement own the group's John Lewis stores and 349 Waitrose supermarkets, as well as an online and catalogue business, a production unit and a farm. Partners share in the benefits and profits, through the annual bonus based on profits. The John Lewis Partnership is one of a growing number of businesses with an employee-owned structure and is a member of the Employee Ownership Association (EOA), the not-for-profit membership body representing the sector.[114] Although changing retail behaviour has forced the closure of eight John Lewis department stores, with a possible eight more on the line, the group has shown itself considerably more robust than high street rivals Debenhams and House of Fraser, emerging from the pandemic as "last man standing among the mass-market department store chains" with sufficient resources to plan an £800 million revamp of the business.[115]

Julian Richer. In May 2019 the owner of Richer Sounds, the home entertainment retail chain, announced that he had transferred 60 per cent of his shares into a John Lewis style trust for the chain's 531 employees. The company paid Richer an initial £9.2m for the stake, but he was due to give £3.5m of that back to staff, who were to receive £1,000 for every year they had worked for the retailer.[116]

Admiral Group. Founded in 1993 and listed in 2004, Admiral, which markets insurance products and loans, has a workforce of over 10,000 and offices in several countries. A policy that favours promoting managers from within has been crucial in maintaining company culture and values. Every day is a dress-down day and there are ping-pong tables and games consoles in office breakout areas. The company also has a dedicated "ministry for fun", which encourages departments to outdo each other with imaginative ways to raise a smile during the working day.[117] Charity fundraising is also a priority. David Stevens, a company founder, says: "One advantage of people enjoying being engaged is we have really good retention. It's hard for someone to steal our best people ... Our staff are genuinely interested in how well the company does." Employees are given shares in the company twice a year. Admiral Group was chosen as the Best Big Company to work for in 2019.[118]

HubSpot. The US software developer has placed employee wellbeing front and centre in its operations, building "a culture of flexibility, learning, and belonging" and helping each employee to be "the best 'you' that you can be, both inside and outside of work". Initiatives include remote working, unlimited leave, month-long sabbaticals after five years, Vacation Quota Relief and a 15 per cent discount on company shares. Perhaps not surprisingly, HubSpot was named Glassdoor's #1 Best Place to Work in 2020.[119]

Aviva. One of the world's largest insurance companies, Aviva has committed strongly to employee wellbeing. "We want our people to be able to enjoy a decent standard of living – that's why we're proud to be a real Living Wage Employer in the UK. And that includes contractors and suppliers who work on our sites too." The company gives employees in the UK, Ireland, France, Singapore and Italy the same entitlement to paid parental leave, regardless of gender, sexual orientation or how an individual became a parent.[120]

Netflix. As a global media company, Netflix actively promotes diversity and inclusion, and has a string of policies designed to achieve work-life balance for employees. It encourages working "smarter, not harder" so that, as an employee, you can take time off "when your mind and body need a break". Staff who become new parents generally take four to eight months. Employees set their own vacation schedule. The company's goal is to "dismantle pay disparities across gender and race".[121]

Canon. Based on its corporate philosophy of *kyosei* (living and working together for the common good), Canon strives to create a workplace environment that fosters mutual respect among its ethnically and culturally diverse workforce. The company maintains a zero-tolerance policy on harassment – defined broadly to include sexual harassment, power harassment, and maternity harassment – and has established a Harassment Hotline across all the members of the Group to provide consultation services.[122]

6. Minimise remuneration differentials within the business

Incentive packages for directors (including cash bonuses and awards of shares) are often defended as the price of achieving high performance and enhanced return to shareholders through dividend payments and increased capital value.

But given that UK FTSE CEOs earn an average of £901.30 per hour (2021 figure), the gulf between directors' earnings and those of the lower-paid employees quickly invites a charge of unfairness and disrespect for their contribution to the success of the business.[123] Rectifying this balance is a powerful statement of intent from directors to the workforce.

Key recommendations:

- **Limit pay differentials**. Former British Prime Minister David Cameron suggested before the General Election in May 2010 a maximum pay differential of 20:1 in the public sector. This was the same pay differential ratio applied by John Pierpont Morgan, founder of JP Morgan bank, in the 19th century. He was concerned that increasing this differential would affect morale and productivity. Before its takeover by Amazon in 2018, Whole

Foods Market, a US company, had a ratio of 19:1 between the highest cash compensation and average employee cash compensation to address what they called 'internal equity'. The company reported that the restriction had not led to the loss of any executive it wanted to retain.[124] It is suggested that the ratio be limited to 20:1 between the highest and lowest employee remuneration, accepting that it may take some years to achieve this by reducing higher levels of remuneration and increasing lower pay levels. This planned approach would be documented, disclosed and explained by the company in its annual report and accounts. The ratio takes account of the fact that higher-paid employees are likely to work significantly longer hours than the lowest paid, and will pay a higher rate of tax.

- **Make deferred bonuses standard**. Require that bonus pay-outs to executives be deferred for a significant period, and subsequently not paid out (or clawed back) if the longer-term performance of the company is poor. The UK Corporate Governance Code requires remuneration schemes to promote long-term shareholdings by executive directors that support alignment with long-term shareholder interests, noting that share awards granted should be released for sale on a phased basis and be subject to a total vesting and holding period of at least five years. EU rules limit bankers' bonuses to the equivalent of their base annual salaries, or to two times their base salaries with the approval of company shareholders.[125] If deferral periods broadly match the duration of a typical risk-cycle, incentives to risk-shift through time are likely to be significantly reduced – as also will be the incentive to set only short-term objectives. A UK government White Paper published in March 2021 recommends a proposal for a two-year clawback to apply in cases of serious misconduct, material misstatement of results, an error in performance calculations or a failure of internal control or risk management.[126]

- **Be transparent in calculations and disclosures.** Ensure that the amounts taken into account to calculate pay differentials include not only normal pay and bonuses but other parts of a remuneration package, for instance pension contributions, health insurance, life policy premiums and vehicle use. To demonstrate that directors and remuneration committees have properly and fairly addressed pay levels throughout a company (or group of companies), disclose pay bands (the number of employees between specified pay levels) and explain what justifies differing levels of remuneration and the policy with regard to pay increases (including pension contributions) in respect of each level.

- **Include all employees as far as possible in the full range of remuneration and benefits.** To encourage parity of treatment between all employees, ensure that rights to shares or the grant of share options are given to executives and all employees on the same proportional differential basis applied to remuneration (before bonus) within the company. Dividends paid to directors and employees, in their capacity as shareholders, would not be regarded as remuneration for the purposes of applying this principle.

- **Engage both shareholders and employees in the approval process for remuneration packages of directors.** As noted earlier, shareholders occasionally vote down proposed remuneration packages. If director pay must be earned in terms of value created for shareholders, however, the same is surely true of employees, whose collective efforts drive company productivity. Giving employees a voice on a company's remuneration committee is an important part of the human connectivity between board and shop floor, and more likely to result in a fair and uncontroversial distribution of rewards.

Companies already engaging with this

Lee Valley Tools. Founder Leonard Lee is a Canadian entrepreneur and innovator who shared his success by paying employees well, giving them part of the company's profits, and making sure they never experienced layoffs. He raised eyebrows in the business community by promising that no executive in his company would make more than 10 times the wage of the lowest-paid worker, a ratio almost unheard of in Canadian industry. True to his commitment, the company has never laid off staff, and 25 per cent of pre-tax profits are paid out to employees each year as a bonus. In an interview with the Globe and Mail in 2013, Leonard Lee commented, "You get tremendous loyalty from employees if they enjoy their work and they are participating in the income and they have the authority that they need to execute their job." Begun as a small mail-order business, Lee Valley Tools now sells about $150 million annually of woodworking and gardening tools, along with kitchen equipment, hardware and clothing. It has 19 retail stores across Canada in addition to its catalogue business, and 850 full-time employees.[127]

Gravity Payments. In 2015 Dan Price, company founder and CEO of Seattle payment processing firm Gravity Payments, took a 90 per cent pay cut and used his company's profits to give his employees a salary increase, pledging that all employees would make at least $70,000 annually in the next three years. To do that he cut his $1 million salary to $70,000, and dipped into the firm's annual $2 million in profits. The move doubled the pay of about 30 of his workers and meant significant increases for an additional 40. Four years later Gravity is reported to have 80 per cent more customers than when Price announced the wage increase. Beyond that, Price's decision has inspired other business leaders to consider the way generous salaries foster employee engagement, which in turn can deliver satisfied customers and clients.[128]

Lloyds Banking Group. A 2017 report by Group Chairman Lord Blackwell aimed to provide "a clear link between remuneration and delivery of the Group's key strategic objectives, namely, becoming the best bank for customers whilst delivering long-term, superior and sustainable returns to shareholders." The report demonstrates that awards for executive directors are determined in the same way as for employees, and details the share options awarded to named individuals. Awards made to executive directors and members of the group executive committee are subject to clawback for at least seven years from the date of grant, extended to ten years where there is an ongoing internal or regulatory investigation.[129]

Samsung. At least since 2012, Samsung has included on its AGM agenda the "Approval of Director Remuneration Limit" for discussion and vote. At the 51st AGM in 2020 the item was passed almost unanimously (the majority exceeding 99 per cent of shareholders voting).[130]

7. Treat suppliers fairly by paying them promptly and giving them support to develop their businesses

A stakeholder approach will regard suppliers as partners rather than members of a pool of dispensable and competing sellers. A supply chain isn't a linear delivery system, but a dynamic value network made up of interacting players. Often a principal supplier will have its own supply chains, meaning that the supply network in aggregate may employ more people than the buying company employs directly. Suppliers may differ in the degree of alignment they want with a customer, especially if they are supplying different companies in the same sector. However, a considered policy towards suppliers is becoming increasingly important, particularly where, as in the UK's Modern Slavery Act 2015, regulations specifically require companies to ensure acceptable behaviour in the suppliers they contract with.

Key recommendations:

- **Ensure that all dealings between the company and its suppliers are transparent, just and fair**, even if the company is much larger and stronger than the other party. Look for long-term alliances that deliver value to both parties. Provide active support to suppliers to develop and protect their business, for instance by helping to improve the quality of their products and, where practical, help with new technology. Develop policies for the awarding of contracts, the negotiation of fair terms, and the method by which contracts are varied or terminated, offering generous periods of notice and, where appropriate, the offer of reasonable compensation for loss to the supplier.
- **Pay on time.** Extend fairness to payment terms by settling accounts at least by the contractually agreed date. Usually there is no good reason why a supplier should not be paid within seven days of the receipt of the goods and invoice. In appropriate cases, invoices can be paid early if the supplier is thought to have cash flow problems. The UK government White Paper mentioned earlier proposes that the annual report states how the company has performed with regard to payment to suppliers during the previous year.[131]

Companies already engaging with this

Levi Strauss & Co. In 2014, the company launched a collaborative financing programme with its garment suppliers in developing countries, many of whom were small and struggled to find affordable financing. When funds were scarce, they would often be forced to take cost-cutting measures that could compromise their workers' health and safety as well as the environment. Levi Strauss & Co. partnered with the International Finance Corporation to provide reliable financing at rates far lower than suppliers could obtain on their own. This gave them the stability they needed to do their best work, simultaneously improving working conditions and benefiting the environment. By treating its suppliers as valued partners, Levi encourages the smaller companies to do all they can to meet the company's environmental, health and safety standards. The programme also gives the suppliers a powerful incentive to do better by linking their financing rates to their "Terms of Engagement" scores. As suppliers continue to improve, the rates continue to drop.[132]

Alpro. Like many of the more than 3,300 companies[133] worldwide qualifying as B Corporations, Alpro, a specialist in whole food solutions, takes supplier relations seriously. Alpro's average relationship with suppliers is 6–9 years, and the company actively monitors the partners it works with for their conduct on a variety of issues including working hours and use of child labour.[134]

Yamaha. The company has an explicit policy on engagement with stakeholders, including suppliers. "We take opportunities to engage in dialog with our stakeholders to hear their opinions and learn what they want, and then apply what we have learned in our corporate activities." Yamaha regards business partners as "traveling with us together on the road toward realising our company philosophy" seeking to "deepen mutual understanding and to maintain and build positive relationships of trust, based on fair and transparent transactions." Means of communication are specified, and include production and sales trend briefing sessions, policy explanation meetings, and questionnaire surveys.[135]

8. Treat customers and the local community fairly

Market forces often encourage companies to be more mindful of their customers than of their suppliers, but the fact that companies depend on persuading customers to buy has sometimes incentivised the use of persuasion techniques that are misleading or disingenuous.

Key recommendations:

- **Seek a reputation for fairness.** Ensure that payment terms with business customers are considered fair by both parties, so that a large company does not take undue advantage of its size and market power. Establish a complaint resolution procedure that is clear and accessible, including information on who to talk to first and the appropriate point of contact if the dispute escalates. Where equipment is involved, minimise both "time to repair" (TTR) and the number of times the company has to send somebody out to do repairs. Also, allow business customers to terminate contracts on terms which give them time to find an alternative supplier.

- **Refuse to encourage irresponsible lending.** Consumer debt – reckoned in the USA to stand at $4.14 trillion as of September 2019,[136] and likely to have risen considerably in the aftermath of Covid-19 – is known to be a huge source of personal stress and ill-health, and a major factor in relationship breakdown which in turn has net negative impact on the wellbeing of children. According to Relate "1 in 5 debt advice clients say debt has a 'considerable' impact on their relationships with their children" – which can involve "children harbouring the financial stress of the family, leading to depression, anxiety and aggression."[137] A business concerned about wider relational stability can simply refuse to encourage the promotion of personal debt through its products and services.

- **Don't hide from customers.** In retail and service provision, keep person-to-person contact at the heart of customer relations. Many sales functions are being efficiently automated (notably by online retailers, insurance brokers, and travel booking services), but customers often have issues that cannot be handled adequately with artificial intelligence. Customers who receive a personal service and whose complaints are handled in a prompt and sympathetic manner are more likely to remain loyal, recommend the company to friends, and to mention it favourably on social media and online reviews.

- **Integrate with the community.** Take active steps to develop relationships in the communities in which the company operates, cutting across racial, religious and ethnic boundaries, not only by the use of CSR funds but by encouraging employees to become involved in community activities and addressing the long-term interests of the community by seeking to ensure job stability and environmental sustainability.

Companies already engaging with this

TalkTalk. On October 21, 2015, TalkTalk, the London-based telecoms company, began investigating a suspected cyber-attack. The attack was accompanied by a ransom demand. The company could not immediately confirm the scale of the breach. The first and most important decision it took was to be honest with its customers, warning them as quickly as possible in order to protect them, even if that risked alarming many who would subsequently turn out to be unaffected. Note that, according to the *New Statesman*, it took British businesses an average of 21 days to submit reports on data breaches to the Information Commissioner's Office. The required timeframe is 72 hours.[138] TalkTalk confirmed the benefits of this approach in the following year's annual report, claiming that the cyber-attack "provided valuable insight and evidence that focusing on existing customers yields significant commercial and reputational benefits. As a result of the honesty and openness with which TalkTalk approached the data breach (including the offer of a free upgrade to all customers in recognition of their loyalty), trust in the brand has increased. Customers are now, on average, more willing to trust, and buy more products from TalkTalk, than they were before the attack."[139]

Swann-Morton. In 1932, before the Sheffield company produced a single razor blade, founders W.R. Swann, J.A. Morton and Miss D. Fairweather drew up four statements to guide their entry into the capitalist world. The first was: "Claims of individuals producing in an industry came first, before anything else, and must always remain first. They are the human beings on which everything is built." The blade manufacturer has a strong commitment to keeping jobs and manufacturing within its Sheffield locale. By doing this, it has protected itself for the longer term through a combination of acquisition and making products it would otherwise have had to import. As one representative of the company put it: "If you can make it in Sheffield, let's make it in Sheffield. If we can make it in Yorkshire, let's make it in Yorkshire. If we can make it in England, let's make it in England."[140]

Nestlé. The company encourages dialogue with stakeholders, and states that "convenings, workshops and other events provide opportunities to deepen that dialogue, building on our understanding of important societal issues" – an interaction which "facilitates collective action and promotes trust and mutual respect." In 2019, Nestlé held a Stakeholders Convening in London, attended by 70 stakeholders as well as the company CEO, two members of the Executive board, and 15 employees. On the agenda were infant nutrition, diversity and inclusion, and plastic packaging, which are of concern to many customers and local communities.[141]

9. Minimise the risk of financial instability to protect the company and its stakeholders

According to *Forbes*, in the forty years since 1980, the level of US corporate bonds outstanding has risen from $468 billion (16 per cent equivalent of GDP) to $10.6 trillion (50 per cent equivalent of GDP).[142] The risks to a company and its stakeholders from over-borrowing are significant, particularly when interest rates begin to rise. The company has to fund interest payments from its pre-tax profits, and will be required to refinance when the debt is due to be repaid. Further, if the company is in financial difficulty, it is likely that the debt will be converted into equity to achieve solvency, substantially diluting the interests of shareholders. Moving away from dependence on debt funding takes time and it would be expected that companies would move gradually to limit borrowing levels.

Key recommendations:

- **Limit debt exposure**. Limit the amount of debt to a level no greater than the amount of the paid-up share capital and reserves of the company (debt including trade creditors and amounts due under finance leases), and report on it at quarterly meetings of shareholders and other stakeholders.[143]
- **Seek shareholder approval for debt financing.** Since some borrowing is always likely to be required due to the difficulty of raising sufficient equity to cover cash flow fluctuations, and may be important to achieving a good credit score, ensure that any increase in

the amount of debt permitted by the company is approved by a resolution of shareholders.

- **Find alternative sources of funding**. Fund expansion of the business by acquisition and investment from profits generated by the operations of the company or from issuing additional shares, rather than taking on more debt, in order to distribute risk more widely.
- **Use relational risk analysis**. When taking on new debt, consider the impact on both the company and its relationship with stakeholders due to the additional risks of that debt on the company's stability.

Companies already engaging with this

Boodles. Owned by the Wainwright family for over 200 years, high-end jeweller Boodles posted pre-tax profits of £5.1m in 2018. Expansion plans have always depended on generating enough income to pay for them. The company has no debt. The operating principle is to keep ownership in the hands of the people who run the company, buying out other investors. The debt-free approach to expansion has kept the business profitable across six generations.[144]

Garmin. Quoted on the NASDAQ and one of the most advanced players in the marine and aviation fields, Garmin is a familiar name thanks to its range of road navigation devices. At the end of first quarter 2020, the company had $1.4 billion in cash and equivalents and no debt. According to CEO Cliff Pemble, "Our balance sheet provides stability to our investors through our commitment to an attractive dividend and allows us to invest for the future when others are pulling back." While acknowledging that the company has not been immune to the impact of Covid-19, he insists that a "strong balance sheet protects businesses in times like these." For years, Garmin has routinely increased research and development spending by between ten and fifteen per cent per annum.[145]

10. Fulfil obligations to wider society

Conflicts of interest between the financial goals of a company and its stakeholder network can be surprisingly obvious. Oil and gas companies like ExxonMobil have funded research that disputes climate change or that links energy taxes to lost jobs. The *New York Times* reports that companies like Coca-Cola and Pepsi have sponsored ostensibly grassroots campaigns to limit taxation on food when, at a time of soaring childhood obesity, and with more than one-in-three adults overweight, health advocates say that soda taxes are an effective way to dampen consumption of sugar-sweetened beverages.[146] Pharmaceutical companies have been accused of increasing profits by pushing for greater access to highly addictive opioids,[147] and internet giants of sharing user information without informed consent.

Against this background, companies focused on relational stability not only ensure a balance of benefit to stakeholders, but also, in an environment of deep public mistrust, help to recover the reputation of the corporate sector as "good corporate citizens".

Key recommendations:

- **Publicly disown tax avoidance.** Pay tax in any particular country in respect of the profits of the business of the company earned in that country. Regard a return of part of the profits of the company as a contribution to the infrastructure and national institutions of the country in which the company operates and on which it relies, as a moral rather than purely legal obligation.
- **Expand understanding of the term Corporate Social Responsibility (CSR).** CSR has a much wider application than normally appreciated. The "Social" in the middle of CSR can be defined to include, amongst other things, customer satisfaction, data protection and privacy, gender and diversity, employee engagement, and human rights. However, even this definition is too narrow. For example, working hours have a profound impact on relationships within families, and whether couples decide to have children. This then affects a country's birth rate which is the key to its long-term existence as a viable independent political and economic entity.

  Public attitudes, and relationships among family and friends, are influenced by whether companies' advertising budgets focus on individual freedom and satisfaction, or how products and services can encourage and sustain family and community relationships; and whether the company prioritises job opportunities for young people to gain work experience and reduce national levels of unemployment. All these considerations should influence board and management decisions.

Local CSR, of course, remains important. Commitments of at least 2 per cent of pre-tax profits should also be made for CSR projects for the assistance of employees in their local communities, or local communities of their suppliers in low-income countries. This indicates the company recognises its social obligations towards communities locally or across the world from which it takes its personnel and makes its livelihood.

- **Engage with poverty in low-income countries**

One of the greatest and most ignored realities of the world in the twenty-first century is the relative poverty of such a large proportion of humanity who live in the Global South. In a relational worldview, these people matter simply because they are human beings, all of whom are of equal value and should be treated with the same dignity, respect and, as far as we are able, with as much compassion as we would show to a next-door neighbour who had fallen on hard times.

A company following the ten points of the Relational Stability Strategy will be benefitting this largely anonymous and yet enormous group of people, both directly and indirectly. Directly, through the attention it gives to its supplier networks, helping companies in low-income countries (LICs) develop their businesses; indirectly, through their commitment to avoid further harm to the global environment. However, companies can do more.

Companies can deliberately choose to place manufacturing facilities in LICs, not just to take advantage of lower labour costs, but to address global income inequalities. Companies can also, through the treatment of their workforce, demonstrate standards of respect to those on low-incomes. This can be done, for example, through levels of pay of low-income employees, training and advancement opportunities of talented individuals, and ensuring no gender discrimination in their policies. In addition, they can motivate investors to recognise the scale of the unfairness involved in the present world order, and encourage them to support the companies in which they invest in their initiatives, and in other ways.

- **Look after the environment.** In the last few years, with environmental issues starting to dominate the news agenda, companies have considerably expanded their commitments in this area. Given the obvious value to companies of being able to demonstrate ESG credentials, it is tempting to set impressive targets which then have to be quietly rowed back in the face of competing priorities and the sheer technical difficulty of reaching targets in time. Commitments should be made, but they should be backed up with sustained action and informed by rigorous research on the effectiveness of the measures proposed (including those aimed at achieving carbon neutrality). Progress towards achieving environmental goals should also be reported regularly.

Companies already engaging with this

Mott MacDonald. A UK-based global consultancy company that manages varied and demanding engineering projects, Mott MacDonald has a long-term strategy of engagement with the community. The company's aim is "to improve society by considering social outcomes in all we do, relentlessly focusing on excellence and digital innovation, transforming our clients' businesses, our communities and employee opportunities." It has resisted takeover attempts and avoided asset stripping, instead focusing on sustainability, organic growth and the long-term benefits for the company and its employees. It also keeps the United Nations' Sustainable Development Goals at the heart of the business.[148]

Amazon. Although subject to allegations of anticompetitive practice and poor labour relations, the global retail giant has taken the initiative on climate change, announcing on 19 September 2019, a commitment to meet the Paris Agreement 10 years early. Amazon's Shipment Zero initiative plans to make every Amazon shipment net zero carbon, with half of all shipments reaching this goal by 2030.[149] Progress rarely moves in a straight line, and critics have pointed out that the company still relies on vast quantities of pulp and paper to package its products, while having no explicit commitment to reduce tropical deforestation. The company's introduction of a new externally-validated certification called Compact by Design in Europe, which identifies products with a more efficient design (including less or lighter packaging) has been described by Mike Childs, head of policy at Friends of the Earth, as "a small step in the right direction".[150]

Vodafone. The rise of "tax shaming" has driven a paradigm shift across the private sector. In 2010 protesters forced the closure of the Vodafone store on Oxford Street, London. Today the company makes an effort to be responsible and transparent in the way it handles tax liability. According to Vodafone Group plc's CFO Margherita Della Valle: "Acting with integrity in the creation and execution of our tax strategy, policies and practices is absolutely core to our approach to tax, as is our commitment to transparency. We disclose our financial contributions to governments at a country level, as we believe this is an important way to demonstrate that it is possible to achieve an effective balance between a company's responsibilities to society as a whole, through the payment of taxes (and other government revenue-raising mechanisms), and its obligations to its shareholders."[151]

Microsoft. Like many big corporates in the era of climate change, Microsoft has placed a strong emphasis on CSR. In 2019, the company donated $1.4 billion to non-profit entities, not counting the $158 million donations from employees and the 700,000 volunteering hours in which 75 per cent of employees participated. In total, Microsoft has reached 19,550 non-profit entities and schools, and is consistently ranked among the corporates with the best CSR initiatives.[152]

"*Why would you invest in a company which is out of sync with the needs of society, that does not take its social compliance in its supply chain seriously, that does nothing about the costs of externalities, or of its negative impacts on society?*"

PAUL POLMAN,
former CEO of Unilever[153]

6. LIMITS OF SELF-GOVERNANCE

As mentioned at the start of the book, reforming capitalism has been high on the media agenda for at least ten years. Leading players in and around business have developed various initiatives, some of whose proposals address stakeholder relationships. All of these initiatives are making a major contribution to change the purpose and practice of companies.

Among the best-known initiatives are these:

- **Certified B Corporations.** These are a "new kind of business that balances purpose and profit" which the B Corporations website describes as "legally required to consider the impact of their decisions on their workers, customers, suppliers, community, and the environment."[154] Over 3,000 companies in over 70 countries have signed up – though at the time of writing the movement represents mainly conscientious private business leaders and has not attracted many listed companies. The UK wing of B Corporations acts as the secretariat for Better Business Act campaign, an initiative aiming to change Section 172 of the Companies Act 2006 (the main provision about the duties of directors in the Act) to advance the interests of shareholders alongside those of wider society and the environment.

- **Good Business Charter.** In the UK, the recently-launched Good Business Charter, supported by the Confederation of British Industry and the Trades Union Council, is a "simple accreditation which organisations in the UK can sign up to in recognition of responsible business practices." It measures behaviour over 10 components: real living wage, fairer hours and contracts, employee well-being, employee representation, diversity and inclusion, environmental responsibility, paying fair tax, commitment to customers, ethical sourcing, and prompt payment. A company must meet all 10 commitments to receive GBC accreditation. As with B Corporations, it is voluntary.[155]
- **Integrated Reporting.** This is promoted widely by the International Integrated Reporting Council (IIRC), whose vision is to "align capital allocation and corporate behaviour to wider goals of financial stability and sustainable development through the cycle of integrated reporting and thinking."[156] It enhances accountability and stewardship for six different forms of capital, one of which includes relational capital.

- **Purposeful Business.** An initiative of the The Future of the Corporation programme, Purposeful Business is conducted by the British Academy, the UK's national academy for the humanities and social sciences. It sees the purpose of business as "creating profitable solutions to the problems of people and planet, and not profiting from creating problems". It proposes "a framework for 21st century business based on corporate purposes; commitments to trustworthiness; and ethical corporate cultures." [157]

- **Responsible Business.** At Oxford University, the Saïd Business School has launched a number of research projects under this title. The projects explore: how ownership relates to the endurance, value, and conduct of corporations; mutuality as a new principle for organising business; the transformation of business practices and leadership to become more purposeful; and the authentic enactment of purpose, linking board objectives to strategy and outcomes.[158] Of particular interest is the Economics of Mutuality started by Mars and now led by the Economics of Mutuality Foundation. A commitment to mutuality by creating value for the business as well as for stakeholders (and not just shareholders) is reflected in the 5 principles of Mars. It is built on the belief that an imbalance between the value that a company creates for itself and the value it creates for others will lead to an unsustainable business.[159]

- **The Purposeful Company.** The Purposeful Company (TPC) Task Force was established in 2015 with the support of the Bank of England to transform British business with purposeful companies committed to creating long-term value through serving the needs of society.[160]

These important and significant initiatives have had a limited effect so far, perhaps because they rely on voluntary adoption. However, regulatory authorities in a number of countries have attempted to define and promote good practice in business through corporate governance codes. Like the private initiatives, these encourage self-regulation, though they may have a variety of inducements behind them, ranging from legislation and regulation to pressure exerted through financial markets. They differ a great deal in their scope and cultural context, ranging from minimal requirements to engage with groups outside the company to a recognition that company prosperity depends on creating value for all stakeholders.

SOUTH KOREA

An example of a country where relatively limited progress has been made thus far on requiring companies to take into account the interests of their stakeholders in their corporate governance is South Korea.

There is no requirement in South Korea for companies to involve or even consult employees in company decision-making. In any event, fewer than 11 per cent of employees belong to trades unions. Further, there is no formal requirement to involve or consult suppliers or major customers in decision-making, although it seems that there is informal consultation with these stakeholders.

Shareholder pressure has grown over the past two years, in particular by the National Pension Service, the largest institutional investor in Korea, which has introduced a stewardship code. There are other shareholder activism movements, in particular over the governance of *chaebol* companies.[161] These are family-controlled conglomerates which dominate South Korean industry and finance. The five biggest chaebol groups alone account for over 50% of the market capitalisation of listed companies.[162] The issues addressed concern the management of these companies, including the election of family members as directors and executives.

In regard to other stakeholders, chaebols generally permit trade unions in their companies. However, Samsung was unusual amongst chaebols in this respect. After prohibiting unions for 50 years, it permitted membership recently but there were only 500 members by November 2019, with an expectation of growth only up to 10,000 members. There are cultural and other reasons for this low number. Other stakeholders tend to have little influence; for instance, the legal system gives little help to suppliers in enforcing rights. They are vulnerable to being removed from the chaebol supply chain with little remedy and few alternative buyers. Furthermore, the increase in the non-regular, non-employee workforce since the economic crisis of 1997, combined with both political and corporate resistance towards collective action and bargaining in the 2000s, have significantly weakened any remaining influence of trade unions.[163]

The Korean Government has recently introduced legislation to encourage shareholders to engage with corporate governance to make company operations more transparent and fair. The Korean Commercial Code was amended in 2020 to cap voting rights to 3%

of their shareholdings for the appointment of audit committee members who are not outside directors. This has limited application as only listed companies with substantial assets are required to have audit committees. There had been plans for this to apply to the appointment of outside directors to audit committees as well, but this was not pursued.

Political moves to apply greater corporate accountability are likely to be introduced by further empowering minority shareholders. Attempts by government to encourage companies to increase dividend payments have often been met by investment of surplus funds in assets which are not central to the business operation in order to avoid an increase in dividends. There are also moves by government to regulate the level of control of *chaebol* companies by family members. However, such moves are controversial. There remains an influential contingent in South Korean politics which favours the close relationship between chaebols and the government.

With growing importance of environmental, social and governance (ESG) issues, however, several Korean conglomerates created a task force team to address ESG issues as part of their corporate management strategies. In this regard, South Korean President Moon Jae-in is also actively encouraging ESG activities and responsible investing, declaring the year 2021 as the "original year" for the expansion of ESG management. The financial authorities in Korea recently unveiled a plan to establish new policy frameworks for ESG management, including the implementation of mandatory ESG disclosures for listed companies, which will be implemented by individual companies on a voluntary basis for the foreseeable future.

THE UNITED STATES

According to Felix Lessambo's review of global corporate governance, "The United States struggles with its corporate governance framework" for reasons that include an excessive concentration of power in the hands of top management, lack of efficiency in prosecuting crimes, and the existence of loopholes engineered by Congress under the mandate of Washington DC lobbyists.[164]

The US has not adopted a corporate governance code for US companies.[165] Company-specific rules for corporations derive from the corporate charter and (to a lesser extent, and with less authority) from corporate bylaws – the latter being subject to change by shareholders.[166] More widely, governance matters are addressed through a combination of state and federal laws and regulations. While this generally comprises a piecemeal regulatory framework, it does include some noteworthy and targeted requirements at the federal level, such as the corporate governance and disclosure control requirements set out in the Sarbanes-Oxley Act.

More than half of US listed companies are incorporated in Delaware, which offers, according to David Brunori, a George Washington University Law School professor and tax expert, "an opportunity to game the system and do it legally." Advantages include the "Delaware loophole" by which certain types of revenue can be declared in Delaware rather than in the state where the business actually occurred.[167]

Although companies listing on the New York Stock Exchange or Nasdaq must abide by the corporate governance requirements in the listing rules, the conversion of exchanges to listed companies has intensified competition between them, calling into question their ability to effectively perform regulatory or corporate governance enhancing functions. However, the exchanges are required to implement certain corporate governance requirements imposed by law, which are partially policed by the US Securities Exchange Commission, and a number of exchange governance requirements mirror federal regulations.

In practice, among the most influential voices in US corporate governance is the US Chamber of Commerce (CoC), which is a lobbying group that represents millions of US businesses that generally supports a regulation-light approach and regularly engages with the SEC on regulatory and governance matters, and the Business Roundtable (BRT). The BRT received significant media coverage in 2019 following its "Statement on the Purpose of a Corporation", and it has the potential to be influential in connection with how companies consider their relationships with and impact on broader stakeholder groups – including customers, employees, suppliers, communities, shareholders – in the coming years. But since the group is composed exclusively of company CEOs, its "best practice" recommendations on corporate governance operate more as a barometer of current corporate concern than as a set of independent regulatory standards. In addition, proxy advisory firms, such as ISS and Glass Lewis, can also be highly influential on certain governance practices for large US companies.

THE UNITED KINGDOM

It is well established in UK company law that, in carrying out their duties to promote the success of the company for the benefit of shareholders (the primary focus), directors must have regard to certain other stakeholder interests, including (in summary) those of employees, suppliers and customers and the impact of the business on the community and the environment.[168] In a recent change to reporting requirements, for financial years which started from January 2019, legislation now requires that large and medium-sized companies/groups with over 250 employees in the UK to make detailed disclosures explaining how directors have had regard to the interests of employees and other stakeholders. This includes how they have kept employees informed of matters of concern, how they have consulted and engaged with them, encouraged their involvement in the company's performance and had regard to their interests, and how this has effected principal decisions taken by the company.[169]

Further, the recently revised UK Corporate Governance Code, which applies to premium listed companies, has signalled a significant change from previous Codes in that it recognises companies' responsibilities to stakeholders other than shareholders and the importance of contributing to wider society. It states, for example, that to succeed in the long-term directors and their companies need to build and maintain successful relationships with a wide range of stakeholders and be responsive to their views. Directors should also ensure there is effective engagement with, and encourage participation from, stakeholders. Engagement with the workforce is encouraged by appointing a director from the workforce, a formal workforce advisory panel or a designated non-executive director.[170]

GERMANY

German industry is distinctive in the influence workers can exert on decision making at the senior level. A stock corporation (*Aktiengesellschaft*) must have a two-tier board structure, with the management board, responsible for the running of the company, appointed, supervised and advised by a supervisory board (*Aufsichtsrat*). In companies with more than 500 employees in Germany on average, one third of the advisory board must consist of employee representatives. Where a company or group has more than 2,000 employees in Germany on average, employee representation on the supervisory board rises to 50 per cent subject to a casting vote of the chairman, a role that the shareholder representatives on the supervisory board can claim for themselves.[171]

This system is not arbitrary. It has its origins in the 19th century, when "iron chancellor" Otto von Bismarck attempted to defuse the threat of socialist revolution by making tentative reforms to welfare laws and company structure. The idea of a two-tier board was imported from the Netherlands, where publicly-traded companies had used them during the 17th century. The resulting model, sometimes called "Rhineland capitalism", obliges directors to consider all stakeholders in corporate decisions, including not just shareholders but employees, creditors, suppliers, and local governments, with a long-term and trans-generational perspective.[172]

SOUTH AFRICA

South Africa, probably the world leader in a "soft law" approach to corporate governance, has an innovative code, developed by the Institute of Directors, which has been updated and revised three times over the last 20 years. The most recent iteration, the King IV Code on Corporate Governance, emphasises a stakeholder-inclusive approach which recognises an interdependent relationship between a company and its stakeholders.[173] According to King IV, a company's ability to create value for itself depends on its ability to create value for others, thus incorporating the African concept of *ubuntu* (broadly translated as "I am because you are; you are because we are") into the way companies are run. The board of directors is therefore to take account of the legitimate and reasonable needs, interests and expectations of all material stakeholders in the execution of its duties, in the best interests of the company over time.

Why voluntary initiatives may not work

Voluntary initiatives, requirements in law and governance codes are important and helpful – but they have three crucial limitations: compliance, consistency, and the willingness of boards to change direction.

Compliance

Certification schemes like B Corps rely on a supportive groundswell of public opinion and the influence of enlightened individuals in the financial services industry, like Larry Fink of BlackRock, who are willing to use their leverage over the boardrooms of large companies.

Even when a code has a degree of legislative support, results can be mixed. Reporting in November 2020 on compliance with the revised UK Corporate Governance Code (2018), the UK's Financial Reporting Council states: "As part of our assessment, we were looking for a high standard of reporting which demonstrated that boards had considered matters beyond process and reassessed issues such as company purpose, culture, and strategy, in order to set them at the heart of governance. Whilst we have found examples of good reporting, overall, we are disappointed with the response to the new Code."[174]

The Code's "comply or explain" approach, which stresses accountability to shareholders and the financial markets, allows some flexibility for companies that may, on some specific details, be unable to comply in full.[175] Nevertheless, the review notes that "The FRC's analysis, together with assessments by third parties, shows that the objective of too many companies is to claim full compliance with the Code, which has led to the 'tick-box' practices we have tried to discourage. Too often companies who are not compliant with the Code, do not declare non-compliance but offer vague explanations, and continue this pattern year on year."[176]

Stock exchanges, who could delist a company for noncompliance – seem reluctant to use this power in practice, particularly where, as in the USA, exchanges themselves are competing for business. In reality, the role of enforcer falls mainly to fund managers and activist investors, who tend to focus on a few specific issues (keeping the functions of CEO and Chair separate, and more recently climate action) rather than taking a broad view of a company's relationships with its numerous stakeholders.

Consistency

Improvements to corporate governance at a global scale are piecemeal and vary in scope and effectiveness. The 2016–20 Trump administration showed how national politics can eclipse the social purpose of capitalism. Exposure to global financial markets may broaden a board's perspective or narrow it onto short-term financial goals. Media attention, so influential in raising awareness of environmental issues, may refocus on other matters of public concern.

The problem is illustrated clearly in the European Union. The EU Action Plan (2012), adopted in 2012, aims to encourage long-term growth-orientated investment with a view to making European companies more competitive and sustainable. Among its provisions are reporting on board diversity, risk management, and executive remuneration, as well as improving the quality of corporate governance reports on a comply-or-explain basis. However, although parliaments in all 28 member states introduced or revised the national corporate governance codes between 2005 and 2015, considerable differences remain.[177] The European Commission Directive 2006/46/EC requires all listed companies to produce a corporate governance statement in their annual report to shareholders, but given the widely differing legal traditions and ownership structures across the EU, the aim is only to provide a framework that encourages convergence between national codes.

The will to act

Boardrooms may not, in the end, have a sufficiently deep and durable commitment or the necessary room to maneuverer to do business a different way, especially in the face of pressure from shareholders preoccupied with short -term financial returns.

Criticism of the way companies operate predates the industrial revolution. Early controversies over, for example, working hours have only gradually been resolved with legislation in many industrialised countries and in some parts of the world have hardly been resolved at all.[178] Discussions about diversifying the purpose of companies away from short-term financial gain should therefore be greeted with caution – simply because, in the end, talk is easier than action that may require companies to challenge not only short-term shareholder interests but a financial system where retirement savings in the form of pension funds, pension insurance contracts and in other vehicles depend on the long-term ability of assets to grow and meet liabilities.

Only relatively recently have pension and other investment funds shown interest in moving outside the status quo. It is perhaps too early to see how persistent this change of sentiment will be. Meanwhile, there is a danger that a certification scheme based on self-assessment across a diverse range of criteria may create the appearance of assertive action without resulting in substantive change. There is also a danger that pressure applied to boards will result in decisions that try to answer investors' ESG concerns without first engaging in a dialogue with other stakeholders.

7. THE ROLE OF GOVERNMENT

Although Chapter Five sets out a list of actions to be considered by company boards, which are in some respects similar to other proposals, relational instability differs from other initiatives in that it offers *a fundamentally different way of understanding the problem.*

> *A relationally stable company is not one that responds only to issues that happen to be a matter of current public concern, but one that sets up and maintains permanently proximate, mutually beneficial and fair relationships between its major stakeholder groups. The approach is not behavioural, but infrastructural.*

For that reason, relational stability standards should not be treated as another kind of ESG (Environmental, Social and Governance) filter allowing investors to identify companies committed to social good (labour safety, corporate board diversity, fair trade, renewable energy, the manufacturing and use of bioplastics). The evidence for ESG funds achieving stronger returns than the wider market is, anyway, reported to be "inconclusive"[179] and, besides the attendant problems of measuring qualitative impacts and achieving consensus on what to measure, there is the concern that ESG labels can be used opportunistically by companies and fund managers to launch investment products, greenwash portfolios, enhance share value, and charge differential fees.[180]

By contrast, relational stability provides a framework within which both companies and governments can undertake strategic reform of the system as a whole. The argument is not that relationally stable companies will always outperform their sectors in the short or medium term, but that intentional maintenance of key stakeholder relationships is likely to create the conditions for long-term prosperity and resilience – whatever global or sectoral markets experience in terms of fluctuations and shocks – not only for the company but for the livelihoods and wellbeing of the stakeholders who depend on it and for the societies within which it operates.

Table 3 summarises this by linking specific benefits – for companies and for government – to the ten principles addressed in Chapter Five. Benefits to companies are shown in orange; benefits to government in blue. Blank squares indicate no direct benefit.

Table 3. A summary of the impact of the ten steps to relational stability on outcomes for companies (orange) and government (blue).

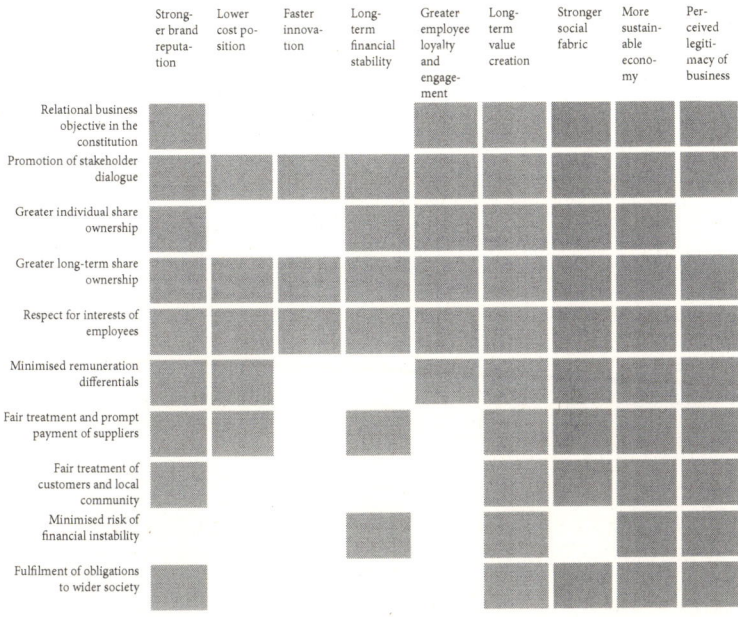

This isn't an appeal for government to impose yet more heavy-handed regulation, but rather to make targeted interventions that alter the relational ecosystem in which companies operate. Government, after all, has a direct interest not only in sustainable wealth-creation but in avoiding the negative externalities of company operations that do substantive damage, attract media scrutiny, and influence public opinion. In addition to which, tackling relational instability in business offers three distinct advantages.

First, by taking a systemic view, it draws attention to the fact that sustainable business is inseparable from sustainable politics and society. The same principles apply to both. Business cannot be asked to compensate for the unsustainable practices of consumers, or for inadequate education, or for manifestos designed mainly to return a party to power. In the end, relational instability affects the entire system.

Second, it does not rely on business people being ethical pioneers but on establishing the conditions for ethical action to become normative. This is crucial, because although some corporate leaders have recently been vocal in their support of social or climate goals, it is uncertain how long this mood will prevail, particularly if against a need to keep the economy growing the business world fails to forge a simple equation between doing good and doing well.

Third, it provides a language with which company directors, investors and government can navigate what, given the events of the last ten years, is likely to prove a critical period for both business and the global economy.

There are a variety of targeted interventions a government might consider, depending on cultural and local economic context. We examine here four possibilities that are particularly relevant to Western nations: changes in the tax regime to rebalance the incentives for equity and debt finance, levelling up competition between large firms and their smaller competitors, favouring reinvestment over simple return to shareholders through dividends and share buybacks, and creating a Relational Stability Authority.

Rebalance equity and debt

Large-scale business depends on transfers between those who provide capital and those who use it. Such transfers are normally effected either through the capital provider buying equity or through the capital user taking on debt. It is debt, however, that nearly all advanced economies incentivise with tax breaks.

Robert Pozen of the Harvard Business School describes this practice as "a senseless subsidy and a candidate for the world's worst economic distortion".[181] It costs governments heavily in forfeited tax revenue, with both Britain and the Eurozone having spent more on subsidies for debt than on defence in 2007.[182] Further, borrowed funds aren't necessarily put to good use. According to British political economist Ann Pettifor, of the $793 billion by which US corporate debt increased in 2015, $700 billion was used for "unproductive, speculative activities".[183]

Additional use of debt to retire equity (for example, financing through buybacks) diminishes equity capital while increasing leverage. As long as the post-tax cost of the debt does not exceed that of equity (which is unlikely), post-tax earnings do not diminish and may well rise. Hence, increased use of corporate debt tends to increase earnings per share (EPS) in the near term, at the greater risk of bankruptcy (and potentially higher cost of debt) in the future. Given that many CEOs' stock options have EPS triggers (especially in the US), they have been incentivised to massage short-term EPS measures higher through additional debt. Hence, US corporate debt-to-GDP levels have risen strongly since the financial crash. A similar, though weaker, effect can be seen in the UK.

Importantly, debt is less relationally stable than equity – which helps to explain the role debt plays in international tension, corporate collapse and personal relationship breakdown, as noted in Chapter Four. The respective needs to access capital and to assure its safe return with interest give lender and borrower quite different priorities. Also, with the increased use of credit rating and automation, lenders neither need nor want to know much more about a borrower than can be gleaned from financial statements or previous payment records. With corporate bonds, debt holders have recently shown themselves willing to buy poor quality bonds at tight spreads with few preconditions on borrower behaviour.[184]

Perhaps most important, debt's inherent asymmetry tends to make it unfair. In general, this is because in a debt relationship borrowers carry most of the risk. Within a company network, the borrowers' risk is passed to shareholders, who will normally be the last in the queue for returns should the company go into liquidation. Also, if a company is in financial difficulty, debtholders may require their debt to be converted into equity as the price for supporting refinancing, leaving shareholder interests substantially diluted. It would not be unusual for shareholders' control of equity to be cut from 100 per cent to 0.5 per cent, leaving debtholders with the lion's share of the benefit if a successful refinancing leads to an increase in the value of the shares. The result is a *de facto* takeover of the company with no consideration paid to those originally invested in it.

Further imbalances appear in the market. Larger companies have greater access to debt finance, and on cheaper terms, than small companies; it is easier to issue and list bonds on the world's stock exchanges when a company's size and asset base gives it preferential access to capital markets as well as economies of scale that result from the lower cost of overseeing large loans. Debt-funded takeovers and private equity buyouts further increase the asymmetry between large and small companies in terms of size and market power. Not least over the last decade, larger companies have benefited disproportionately from quantitative easing (QE).

This applies when central banks bid for and buy their bonds, thereby directly reducing their cost of borrowing (either through the central banks buying the bonds when issued rather than in the secondary market or by reducing yields for future bond issues.) As corporate bonds are illiquid and infrequently sold, the central bank is unlikely to sell the bonds until maturity. Hence, they act as an anchoring holder that won't push yields up when bonds would otherwise sell off. That the central bank holds a company's bonds will also help accessing bond markets in the future at lower yields and may even benefit their credit rating. This is an anti-competitive measure in favour of the privileged companies by the central bank. Smaller companies which do not have access to QE as a means for their debt to be held by central banks are left more vulnerable to future financial shocks.

One way to encourage equity financing is to create greater equality in the tax treatment between debt and equity finance. At the moment, in the UK at least, interest payments are normally exempted from the assessment of taxable profit, whereas equity payments, in the form of dividends, are not. And yet in principle equity is more relationally stable than debt, creating alignment between stakeholders, creating time and incentive to benefit from mutual knowledge, and generally giving investors and directors more equal exposure to the risks of failure and the rewards of success. An investor may be willing to support a business through a difficult period of trading, whereas creditors have little reason to take a long-term view on the merits and value of the underlying business, as their main concern is only that the company remains solvent and able to pay interest and repay principal.

The argument that debt should not be favoured over equity was advanced by some economists as long ago as 1958.[185] As shown in Table 4, equity funding appears on the company balance sheet as an asset rather than a liability. Other things being equal, a company using equity funding will pay corporation tax from a higher net income than a debt-funded company, and thus achieve higher profitability. Were an equity-funded company permitted to deduct dividend payments from pre-tax profit, in the way that debt-funded companies can deduct interest payments, the effect would be to enhance profitability still further, as less tax would be paid.

Table 4. Comparative effect of debt financing and equity financing on the balance sheets and profitability of a company paying UK corporation tax.[186]

The statement of financial position (or balance sheet) shows a company's assets and liabilities at a specific date. The resultant net assets are equivalent to the combined capital and accumulated reserves, i.e. 'equity' or 'shareholders' funds'.

When a company takes on debt, there is no change in its net assets: the inflow of cash increases the company's assets, while the recognition of the obligation to repay the lender increases the company's liabilities. The cash can be used for the intended purpose; the liability remains until it is extinguished by a payment to the lender.

Alternatively, a company may raise funds by issuing new shares. The injection of fresh capital is this way results in an increase in the company's net assets and equity: assets increase due to the inflow of cash; equity increases in recognition of the additional capital put in by the shareholders.

These alternative funding mechanisms can be illustrated by statements of financial position 'before' and 'after' the financing:

	Debt financing		Equity financing	
	Before	After	Before	After
	£m	£m	£m	£m
Sundry assets and liabilities	100	130	100	130
Loan	-	(30)	-	-
Net assets	100	100	100	130
Share capital	20	20	20	50
Accumulated reserves	80	80	80	80
Equity	100	100	100	130

The two alternative funding models not only result in differing balance sheets. They also give rise to differing effects on the profitability of the company (other things being equal). This can be illustrated by comparing the income statements (or 'profit and loss accounts').

	Debt-financed company		Equity-financed company	
	Before	After	Before	After
	£m	£m	£m	£m
Income before loan interest	80	80	80	80
Loan interest	-	(10)	-	-
Income before tax	80	70	80	80
Tax	(16)	(14)	(16)	(16)
Income after tax	64	56	64	64

In the debt-financed company, loan interest reduces the company's income (profit) compared to the equity-financed company. The reduced income results in a lower tax charge and a lower post-tax income.

A further way to reduce indebtedness by companies (in addition to the wider economy) would be to remove the artificial subsidies enjoyed by commercial and investment banks. Bank balance sheets are intrinsically fragile across three dimensions. They are: highly leveraged (holding little capital for the size of their assets); inherently illiquid (holding long-term, hard-to-sell assets funded through short-term deposits and other debts); and systemically vulnerable (holding similar assets to other banks and the liabilities of each other). Hence, the failure of one could result in the failure of many, or all. As a result, governments and central banks try to ensure that confidence in the banking system as a whole is bolstered through various subsidy channels. These include: guaranteed borrowing facilities at the central bank; free (or cheap) deposit guarantees; and implicit "too big to fail" bailouts at taxpayers' expense. In addition, banks are permitted to operate with little capital to keep the cost of debt low. The result is that banks, especially big banks, are subsidised relative to other sources of debt (such as credit unions, decentralised financial institutions and bond markets) and that debt is significantly cheaper than it should be if the risks its production creates were properly priced and insured against.

The relational instability of banks and indebted companies could be addressed by the removal or reduction of these subsidies. This could include ring-fencing guaranteed bank deposits from their risk-taking activities, introducing stringent capital requirements for larger bank balance sheets[187] and setting a maximum size of a single bank's balance sheet relative to an economy to ensure that no institution is "too big to fail". In addition, banks would also lose the tax break for debt finance along with other corporates, thereby reducing the incentive to operate at low levels of capital.

Level-up competition

Relationally stable competition isn't a mechanism by which larger competitors eat up the small. Rather, since the market itself is seen as a way to promote general wellbeing, it requires rules and overarching objectives to which all participants can agree. This alignment is essential, even if the degree of mutual knowledge between participants has to be limited by considerations of commercial sensitivity and patent protection.

Fairness, already a familiar concept in markets, is seldom consistently applied. One reason for this may be the preferential access to debt finance enjoyed by larger companies, as explained above. Another is progressively shifting technology. With the shift to e-commerce, for example, nearly all major retailers have started online operations, but in Europe and North America the sector has been increasingly dominated by Amazon, whose AI/robot-driven, highly-integrated, highly efficient service provides speed, choice and convenience to consumers at a level few others can match.

Size has given large online retailers legitimate advantages through economies of scale in buying power and central administration, at the same time as enjoying the serendipitous boost of a pandemic by which many smaller competitors have been disabled. Online shopping is simply better adapted to survive the challenging Covid-19 environment.[188] The odds are further stacked against traditional retail by business rates (or non-residential property tax), which force high street retailers to operate from a substantially higher cost base because shops occupying prime real estate in city centres will pay higher rates than companies with out-of-town distribution centres. Governments have responded by starting to tax digital services. In 2020, the UK government imposed a new Digital Services Tax (DST) on businesses that provide social media services, search engines or on-line marketplaces to UK users, taxing the portion of profit derived from UK users at a rate of 2 per cent if a group's revenues exceed certain thresholds.[189] The European Union has proposed DST across member states at a rate of 3 per cent on gross revenue for e-commerce retailers located outside their jurisdiction.[190]

More widely, there is an argument for rethinking regulation around company mergers and acquisitions (M&A). The current general presumption is that an acquisition (under UK competition law) should be allowed unless it would be likely to result in a substantial lessening of competition.[191] Unfortunately, contested takeovers can be motivated by managerial desires to aggrandise their position and increase their pay rather than improve efficiency. The upshot is that market concentration has continued to rise (particularly in the IT and banking sectors). This may well be a contributory factor for why productivity growth in high-income countries has stagnated as inefficient large incumbents are protected by regulation, subsidised debt and the relative ease of acquiring smaller competitors.

To promote smaller company size and greater competition, the policy with regard to M&A should be reversed: that is, M&As are not permitted unless they are justified by positively enhancing competition or can be shown to be in the interests of all stakeholders rather than just shareholders. This would also apply to debt-financed acquisitions by private equity companies, although the removal of the tax subsidy to debt (see above) should make these far less prevalent. The focus of directors and managers would then be fixed on profitable, organic, long-term growth rather than buying competitors or worrying about becoming a takeover target if short-term profitability or the share price dips.

Favour reinvestment of surplus funds

In May 2021, Diageo, owner of the Johnnie Walker and Guinness, announced the restart of its pandemic-hit programme to return £4.5 billion of what chief executive Ivan Menezes called "excess cash" to investors through share buybacks or special dividends.[192]

There are valid reasons for a listed company to buy its own shares. Surplus cash reserves can reduce earnings per share, as the return on the cash is lower than on trading activities. A buyback might then increase future earnings per share and enhance the market price. Similarly, the directors may consider that the market price of the shares does not reflect the value of the company's balance sheet assets (for instance in the case of a property investment company) and use a buyback to increase the market price of the remaining shares.

Nevertheless, when companies return cash to investors, they reduce the liquidity they may need when sales and profits drop in an economic downturn, or the funding that could go into research and development, and the opportunity to expand the knowledge and skills of its employees. In 2018, only 43 per cent of companies in the S&P 500 Index recorded *any* research and development (R&D) expenses, with only 38 companies accounting for three-quarters of R&D expenditure.[193] It has been pointed out that McDonald's could pay all of its 1.9 million workers almost $4,000 more a year if the company redirected funds spent on buybacks to workers' pay cheques.[194]

Regimes differ in the way buybacks are regulated. UK listed companies may buy back their shares by purchase on the market if there is authority from the shareholders by resolution, but the purchase must be made out of the distributable profits of the company or out of the proceeds of a fresh issue of shares made for the purpose of financing the purchase. In the USA, by contrast, buybacks have been virtually unregulated since 1982, surpassing dividends as a mode of distributing corporate cash to shareholders in 1997 and recently reaching record volume. Between 2010 and 2019, according to Federal Reserve data compiled by Goldman Sachs, US corporations spent $3.8 trillion buying their own stocks – more than every other type of investor (individuals, mutual funds, pension funds, foreign investors) combined.[195] Just in 2018, with corporate profits riding high on the back of the Tax Cuts and Jobs Act (2017), companies in the S&P 500 Index together spent $806 billion on buybacks –

about $200 billion more than the previous record set in 2007.[196]

Although the level of share repurchase as a proportion of operating profits is significantly lower in the UK (broadly comparable to Australia and Canada, but higher than in Germany), the US has commensurately lower dividend payouts, so overall shareholder payouts are said to be little different between the two regimes. Dividends are less volatile than share buybacks, and more clearly represent a reward to shareholders for holding shares as opposed to selling them. Nevertheless, because both raise the question of fairness across the wider network of stakeholders, it is important to ask what else surplus funds could be used for.

In the interests of wider economic stability, there is a case for governments to encourage companies to retain sufficient cash holdings to facilitate reinvestment in the capabilities necessary to sustain the corporation and that do not disproportionately favour short-term investors (including investment banks and hedge funds) over longer-term stakeholders. Measures might include requiring shareholder rather than board approval (where not already required) or requiring immediate disclosure, thus restricting the participation of insiders who may benefit by buying equity before a buyback is announced. Further, there may be no good business case for incurring debt simply to make a cash payout. [197] A better use of surplus funds in many cases may simply be to pay down debt.

Larry Fink, Chairman and CEO of BlackRock, summed up some of the concerns about distributions to shareholders while underinvesting for long-term growth in the company, in a letter in 2015 to the CEOs of companies in which BlackRock invests on behalf of clients: "As I am sure you recognize, the effects of the short-termist phenomenon are troubling both to those seeking to save for long-term goals such as retirement and for our broader economy. In the face of these pressures, more and more corporate leaders have responded with actions that can deliver immediate returns to shareholders, such as buybacks or dividend increases, while underinvesting in innovation, skilled workforces or essential capital expenditures necessary to sustain long-term growth."[198]

Create a Relational Stability Agency

A Relational Stability Agency (RSA) can be set up in any country or supranational territory to act as an independent non-government public body charged with enhancing the quality of the relational environment in which a country's major institutions, including businesses, operate. This can be done, in particular, by applying the Relational Stability Strategy for Business (based on the principles outlined in Chapter Five) as its core set of standards and would target the preservation and enhancement of human connectivity across economic networks. In the UK it could be established alongside the UK Corporate Governance Code by the Financial Reporting Council or by the Audit, Reporting and Governance Authority when it is formed. A summary of the function, structure, aims and approach of the RSA is set out in Table 5.

Table 5. The nature and responsibilities
of a Relational Stability Agency

Function	• Preserve and enhance human connectivity across economic networks, in particular connecting companies to their stakeholders
Structure	• Independent non-government body supervised (in the UK) by FRC or ARGA
	• Coordinated with regulatory bodies
Aims	• Ensure that all companies take appropriate and transparent action to maintain human connectivity in their relationships with stakeholder groups
	• Create a business environment in which protecting stakeholder interests, and involving stakeholders in business decisions, is regarded as normative
	• Promote the pursuit of relational stability both to realise the social purpose of companies and to increase their efficiency, productivity and profitability
Approach	• Provide ongoing and transparent public reporting on the relational stability of companies, with recognition for excellence
	• Advise companies on measuring and improving relational stability in their stakeholder networks
	• Oversee the development and application of effective metrics to quantify human connectivity in the relationships between stakeholder groups
	• Provide research and training and monitor the quality of reporting by companies

Fundamental to the RSA's responsibility would be to encourage compliance with the standards of the Relational Stability Strategy for Business underlying Chapter Five of this book, both for existing companies (listed and private) and for merged company groups created by takeover. To encourage listed and other large companies to work towards relational stability in their management and operations, the RSA would measure and report publicly on the extent to which they adopt and comply with the principles set by the Strategy.

Initial assessment of levels of compliance would be made using published information, in particular a company's annual report and accounts. The company would be invited to comment on the draft assessment, and these comments would be taken into account in delivering the final rating which could be expressed as a relational stability score, allowing the use of a "kitemark" on company communications if a sufficient level has been achieved. For larger listed companies, achieving compliance might take time, and in these cases the company would give a public statement of its intent to conform to the principles in the Strategy within a five-year period.

Companies would be expected to comply both with the letter and the spirit of the Strategy. The results of the assessment would be updated biennially, such that companies in particular sectors of the economy could be ranked and compared. The RSA might also employ different kinds of ranking, for example by amount of tax paid as a proportion of turnover and profits. The most relationally stable companies would be recognised and rewarded as public benefactors, with a recommendation that high rates of compliance with the principles in the Strategy be tied to lower rates of corporation tax.

"*In 1860–1917 the global economy was reshaped by the rise of giant new industries (steel and oil) and revolutionary new technologies (electricity and the combustion engine). These disruptions led to brief bursts of competition followed by prolonged periods of oligopoly. The business titans of that age reinforced their positions by driving their competitors out of business and cultivating close relations with politicians. The backlash that followed helped to destroy the liberal order in much of Europe.*"

"The superstar company: A giant problem",
The Economist, 17 September 2016

8. THE RELATIONAL STATE

So far this book has examined relational instability in companies and asked how this can be addressed. But, as already indicated,

> companies do not operate in a vacuum. The networks they are part of organically connect them to the rest of society, and relational instability exists not just in companies but in all forms of social organisation, including hospitals, schools, electorates, media, families, communities and government itself. A country may be relationally unstable in much the same way as a corporation.

The purpose of this chapter is to turn from companies to four other main components of a capitalist-democratic society that tend to transmit relational instability, and to indicate what government policy directions might help mitigate or reverse this effect. As in the corporate world, the aim is not to approach human behaviour directly by way of making moral appeals, but to rewire national society through strategic and structural reforms.

The problems of the unrelational state

Besides the operation of the economy, there are four features of democratic capitalism that tend to reduce human connectivity and make a society more relationally unstable: the numerical limitations of democracy; the way in which work is allowed to dominate allocations of time; the tendency to treat labour as a production cost rather than an associate; and the unique emphasis the liberal tradition places on individual rights and freedoms.

POLITICAL POWER: Numerical democracy

Democracies are relationally stable to the degree that they are seen to ensure fair distribution of power. But they also rely on alignment and mutual knowledge. If there is underlying disagreement on the rules by which elections are won, doubt as to the value of the process itself, or an inability to deliver impartial and reliable information effectively to every part of the electorate, the political process will be distorted.

The 2020 US presidential election was, in this sense, conducted on the back of considerable relational risk. The long-term erosion of fairness – seen in the perception that a majority-Democrat Washington elite had, for example, profited by letting American jobs be outsourced to China – helped undermine not only respect for the liberal media but belief in the impartiality of the electoral process itself. Instead of building meaningful mutual knowledge between Democrats and Republicans, the emerging social media environment locked voters into opinion-reinforcing echo chambers while simultaneously exposing them to the unregulated propaganda efforts of mischievous or hostile third parties.[199] There was also a critical loss of alignment. Both sides of the political divide professed loyalty to supposedly unifying national symbols (America, the Constitution, the Flag) but ascribed quite different meanings to them.

All of this overlaid more familiar weaknesses.

First, democracies suffer simply from scale. Large, politically centralised countries inevitably have large numbers of people represented by a single individual,[200] and the more this is the case, the more likely it is that central government will seem remote to those on the fringes, further weakening the perceived legitimacy of decisions made at a level far from the life of the ordinary citizen. This tends to reduce electioneering to a media-led, market-research-driven numbers game. It also creates the space in which political candidates must by necessity be media products; in which the use of social media can mobilise power bases outside the traditional party-political structure; in which well-funded corporate lobbies can influence policy; and in which powerful vested interests may seek to argue that democracy itself is a threat to national cohesion.

Second, democracies often create a carousel of party governments, policies and ministers. Even where institutions and offices remain formally linked, the regular replacement of office-holders can produce the systemic equivalent of hot-desking. Every time ministers change, personal relations with senior civil servants have to be rebuilt. And the differing timeframes of government and civil service – the one driven by election cycles or cabinet reshuffles, the other usually working to longer-term objectives – can create friction and resistance rather than constructive alignment, particularly if successive governments (as they are prone to do) reorganise departments in line with changing policy.

An extension of this problem is that decision-making networks like governments may not be wired to include the most useful relationships, or to create appropriate degrees of transparency, or to access vital information in real time, or to process urgent tasks with the necessary speed. When we face so many rapid and profound changes (the proliferation of advanced weaponry, rising sea levels, more extreme weather events, the growth of new and heavily disruptive technologies in the form of genetics, robotics, and artificial intelligence), it is sobering to reflect that the procedural mechanisms through which leaders are selected, confer, debate and make decisions are not far different from those in use when European governments failed to prevent a regional disagreement between Austria and Serbia turning into a world war.

TIME: The centrality of work

Demands made on an individual's time by commercial networks – particularly through a long-hours culture and the shift to a gig economy that may involve restrictive zero-hours contracts with low wage inflation – have a measurable adverse impact on human connectivity in family and community. Unlike money, the amount of time possessed by any individual is finite. Time can be spent at work only at the expense of time available for other purposes.

The *UK Working Lives Survey* (2019) of 5,136 employees across the UK, published by the Chartered Institute of Personnel and Development, revealed "an epidemic of long hours, stress and poor work-life balance ... with many admitting their job made it hard to switch off in their downtime and caused disruption to their family life." Sixty per cent said they worked longer hours than they wanted to. Twenty-four per cent worked at least ten hours per week more than they had contracted to. Twenty-six per cent said their job affected their personal commitments.[201]

Time itself, of course, is fundamental to mutual knowledge: it takes time to get to know someone, and the less time is made available for this, the harder it becomes to build understanding and friendship. Pressure on working hours, to which may be added a lengthy commute, can easily place personal and work goals in opposition. Issues of fairness quickly arise over the allocation of time in a family (overtime squeezing out the school play). They also arise vertically in a pay structure, because those at the bottom often have less free time and less discretion over its use than those at the top. Excessive demands on personal time routinely show up in statistics of mental health and workplace absenteeism.[202]

Less obviously, but more significantly for government in the long term, commercial pressure on time can produce a long-term impact on the national economy. Where people have insufficient time to form and maintain family relationships, and particularly where this combines with changing social attitudes and the widespread availability of birth control, the result will be a reduction in the number of children being born. Figure 7 shows how over the last 60 years birth rates in many countries, especially in Europe, North America and East Asia, have declined to below replacement levels (average 2.07 births per woman), meaning that populations are starting to shrink, entering a multi-decade phase where the old outnumber the young.

In the context of rapidly rising global population growth, this may seem a minor problem. At the national level, however, it quickly becomes critical when workforce depletion runs ahead of the economy's ability to automate crucial tasks. This has downstream consequences for extended family support networks, workforce resilience and availability, and levels of taxation required to fund state social care. In a world of around eight billion people, the challenge of managing demographic decline may soon be as urgent as that of tackling climate change.

Consider China, where retirement ages, pinned to earlier, shorter life spans, are 50 for blue collar women workers and 60 for most men. "At one end of the demographic spectrum fewer babies are being born and young adults are entering the world of work later; at the other end workers are rushing to take their state pensions at what most Western societies would regard as middle age."[203] On current trends, by 2050 there will be three times as many elderly people in China as there are children. Faced with the prospect of critical labour shortages in industry and the armed forces, the Chinese government is pondering the deeply unpopular move of raising the retirement age – a move that in Russia dropped President Vladimir Putin's popularity ratings from the high 70s to under 48 per cent. Meanwhile, prompted by the latest census data, Beijing has announced that couples will now be allowed to have three children instead of two.[204]

Figure 7. Selected birth rates 1960–2019
(EU figures include the UK until 2017).

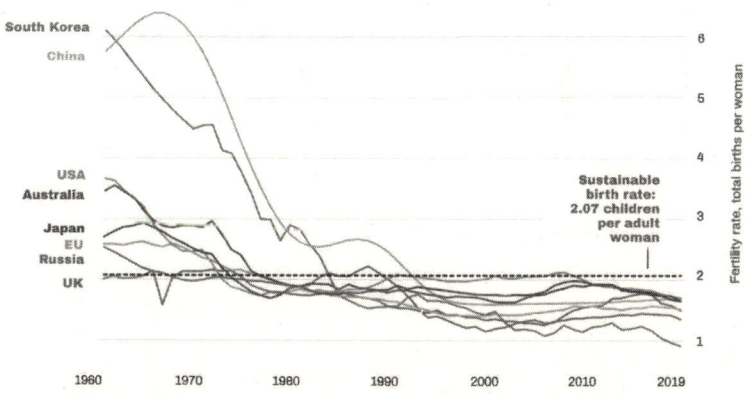

As one leading UK newspaper headline put it in 2021, "It's time we thought more about procreation."[205] Without intervention by government, a progressive decline in the working age population may start to trigger economic stresses – diminishing national revenue, currency depreciation, declining credit ratings, increased cost of government borrowing, loss of inward investment. These in turn will make relational stability even harder to achieve if damage to perceptions of fairness, through resulting tax rises and shrinkage of public services, weaken national consensus and foster civil unrest.

Policy responses can themselves be relationally unstable. Some countries, including Germany, have tried to meet the approaching labour shortage by encouraging immigration. In the short term, this may help support GDP. But the strategy carries risks. Immigrants are, by definition, strangers to the national culture who may not easily integrate. And there can be political repercussions if indigenous communities feel themselves unfairly treated in real or perceived competition for housing, education, healthcare and jobs.

ECONOMICS: Labour as a cost of production

In neoclassical economic theory, labour is regarded principally as a resource and cost of production, required to redistribute itself geographically to match changing patterns of economic growth. This is a doctrine embedded in the EU Single Market which seeks to guarantee free movement of goods, capital, services, and labour across all member states.

Capital, though, is more fluid and adaptable than labour. The Welsh mining industry reached peak output in 1913 and endured a steady decline after World War II as UK energy markets switched to North Sea oil and gas. In its heyday, according to a 2017 study, "Coal owners made huge profits, employment grew, inward migration soared and new pits spread along the Valleys." However, "the final closure of collieries had a heavy and detrimental impact on the prosperity, health, and well-being of those remaining."[206] The same report highlights "the inability of policy to offset the social impacts of industrial decline" – a story that will sound familiar in many older and formerly prosperous industrial regions around the world.[207]

The drag-effect of capital on population is visible nationally in the form of urbanisation (with 68 per cent of the world forecast to be living in cities by 2050[208]) and internationally in migration flows between low-income and high-income countries.

At both levels it tends to create relational instability.

Within high-income economies, there is a general pressure for people to relocate if they want to climb the career ladder. In a recent poll of 2,800 US workers, 62 per cent declared themselves willing to relocate for a new position.[209] The impact of this mobility on local relational stability can be severe. Personal networks become less cohesive. Close relationships between generations are stretched when working-age adults move away – an effect that social media and online video communications can only mitigate.[210] Nuclear families separated from grandparents become more reliant on state or private childcare. Elderly parents feel deprived of family support. Children separated from working parents are more prone to experience lack of motivation, learning difficulties, addictions and depression.[211]

Internationally, migration flows affect not only personal and community wellbeing but the viability of entire regions. The fact that, according to the UNHCR in 2016, about half of the refugees reaching Europe from Syria had university degrees,[212] is another way of saying that a needy region is suffering a skills deficit as well as the impact of war. Economic migrants are often young, male, entrepreneurial and educated, meaning that receiving nations benefit from their training and earning power while the places they leave experience a corresponding loss. In addition, as noted in the previous section, bringing migrants in as cheap labour (often on temporary contracts and with more limited rights and protections than nationals) can provoke discontent by creating unfair competition and undercutting wages.

Such issues tend to be regarded as a regrettable but unavoidable cost of pursuing economic efficiency. But if labour itself is a form of capital – a store of value – there is a strong case for saying that it should be actively conserved and reinvested, especially if the key to corporate as well as national economic growth is invention and innovation. Otherwise, where the economic cycles are long, as with the Welsh coal industry, the shift of financial capital towards new technologies can leave a trail of social damage as the sometimes vast communities built around an industry become geographically remote and economically peripheral. Unemployment rises and workers find themselves unable to move or simply too old to adapt and retrain. Former industrial powerhouses, like the Rust Belt of the United States, turn into areas of deprivation and unemployment, with potentially major consequences for the health of wider society.

SOCIETY: Individualisation

Western democracy and capitalism have developed within a culture that places unique value on freedom and equality.

This has brought immense benefits, in part because freedom of expression and equality before the law are often experienced as fairness. In terms of overall relational stability, however, the advantages are less clear. The trend has been rather towards individualisation: treating people as decision-making units in (usually) very large-scale networks.

In commerce, advertisers micro-target consumers and those in their personal networks (often children) who influence buying decisions. In entertainment, television channels have proliferated in an attempt to capture portions of a market that can be segmented with ever greater precision, while online services like Netflix are leading a charge to delink programming from shared schedules and make it instead a resource to fit individual leisure time.

In finance, the functionalities around banking, investment, insurance and taxation have migrated online, to be accessed by the individual's phone or laptop, driven by the institutions' requirement to achieve accuracy, speed, accountability, a smaller carbon footprint, lower labour costs, and greater user convenience.

In education, the international Programme for International Student Assessment (PISA), recognised as a valuable tool for comparing the success of different national education systems, focuses narrowly on assessments of an individual student's ability in reading, mathematics and science, and frames success mainly in terms of individual competence, economic contribution, earning power, and wellbeing.[213]

Unsurprisingly, relational stability tends to be low in mass, individualised societies where routine transactions no longer require actual meeting. Mutual knowledge gets filtered through electronic media (Facebook, Twitter, internet). What motivates one group or person may be different from what motivates those in the wider network. And, while markets may respond to trends in consumer demand, one person can easily feel isolated and disempowered because individuals in a large system are visible mainly in aggregate: they are members of interest groups, within a national or international pool, which must compete for attention, respect, and a share of resources.

In the Western tradition, the individual's wellbeing is defended by rights established in law. But rights do not change the underlying dynamics of individualisation. They attempt to protect the interests of an individual or stakeholder group by imposing obligations on the rest of society rather than by addressing the quality of the networks connecting them.

The Universal Declaration of Human Rights thus sets out a "common standard of achievement" and requires "every individual and every organ of society" to "strive by teaching and education to promote respect." It does not solve the problem of competing claims for finite resources, leaving the European Court of Human

Rights to temper the right to life by interpreting it "in a way which does not impose an impossible or disproportionate burden on the authorities." Nor does it promote dialogue or the seeking of common ground as a way to resolve conflicting claims, advocating instead the route of adjudication through arbitration or the courts.[214]

Where disputes divide society and no agreed means of adjudication exists (as was the case with Brexit[215]), parties can find themselves violently at odds, with little incentive to further mutual knowledge, no context of common goals within which to settle competing claims, and driven to provocations that only deepen the sense of unfairness felt by both sides.

In general, and essential as it may be as a defence against oppression, a rights culture on its own can easily become combative and litigious. In the US, litigation funding, where a third party, with no direct interest in the proceedings, finances the cost of litigation in return for a share of the claim proceeds if the litigation is successful, is now emerging as a mainstream asset class with an estimated return on investment of 36 per cent.[216] The same practice is growing in the UK – a litigation funder recently agreed to back a £250 million negligence claim against KPMG for its audits of collapsed contractor Carillion plc.[217]

Perhaps the strongest impact of individualisation has come through IT. Even more than the invention of printing, social media has radically changed the individual's role in the global mega-community. By connecting individual strangers interactively and *en masse*, social media both extends and weakens mutual knowledge, "disrupting human discourse, while giving the 'feeling' that we are communicating more than ever."[218] It empowers potentially vast new alignments by linking those who share a common interest. It both equalises access to information and is deeply unfair at a systemic level by making public opinion vulnerable to a relatively small number of powerful players – political, economic, technological – whose motives and actions may remain hidden from view.

Often the driving force is financial. Because there is no market for truth, advertising revenue becomes untethered from news production, leaving traditional news sources, with their known biases and professional journalistic standards, struggling to compete. Money gravitates instead towards what is popular. When attention is currency, the sensational trumps the true. Individual grievance resonates in chatrooms that incubate anger and animosity.[219] Unverified claims gain perceived legitimacy simply by being passed on in sufficient volume and with sufficient speed. As a result, governments and electoral campaign managers now navigate a world in which commercial interests do not always align with the dull and complex business of distinguishing fact from fiction. In the words of Amy Webb, founder of the Future Today Institute, "It's good for democracy to stop the spread of misinformation, but it's bad for business."[220]

Relational stability as a basis for national strategy

Relational stability is the foundation of capital growth – financial, social, intellectual, physical, and environmental. It starts, not with market forces or social classes, but by pointing to the fundamental role of relationships in helping individuals, organisations and societies flourish. In this way, the good society is one defined, not by abstract ideals, but by how it connects its members. It sees that a person is never autonomous but is necessarily born into and shaped by relationships; thus, relationships become the focal point for the description of political and institutional structures, and the unit of analysis for economic and social change.

Relational stability lies at the heart of a sustainable social contract between government and people. Up to a point, because relational stability requires fairness rather than formal equality, marked differences in wealth and power can exist in a society as long as they have an accepted rationale (divine order, seniority, merit, hard work, the general good) and are counterbalanced on the part of an elite by social grace or generosity. But only up to a point. The massive wealth differentials of Tsarist Russia (combined with the impact of rapid industrialisation and a ruinous war) led by degrees to a revolution that shaped European and world politics for much of the twentieth century. Similarly, two hundred years after emancipation, the relational instability of colonial economies, reliant on slavery and indentured labour, and perpetuated in a lingering shadow of prejudice, discrimination and disadvantage, is still capable of fuelling passionate protest, as indicated by the defacing and destruction of public monuments in 2020 in Virginia, Bristol and Belgium.

But if the past cannot be undone, the future can be rewired. Curiously, in light of recent disagreements, the first architects of the post-war European political order were using relational stability in all but name when they established the European Coal and Steel Community (ECSC) at the Treaty of Paris in 1951. Steelmaking – the bedrock of the twentieth-century arms industry – would now become a joint venture governed by a single shared institution in which all six founding member states were aligned. In the words of French foreign minister Robert Schuman, the ECSC was designed to "make war not only unthinkable but materially impossible." Alongside the ECSC, efforts were made to increase mutual knowledge by a policy of twinning towns in France, Germany and the UK that had suffered damage during the war. And the EU embraced a principle of subsidiarity that, at least in theory, ensures fairness between levels of government, such that "in all cases, the EU may only intervene if it is able to act more effectively than EU countries at their respective national or local levels."[221]

Seventy-five years of peace in Europe is no mean achievement. But the weaknesses of today's EU reflect a failure to follow through on tackling relational instability. According to current EU law, subsidiarity "does not mean that action must always be taken at the level that is closest to the citizen."[222] A thriving tourist industry has only partially overcome the region's language and cultural barriers. The rigid membership terms of the euro has advantaged core states at the expense of peripheral ones like Greece. And the perception of Brussels as, in David Cameron's words, "too big, too bossy, too interfering,"[223] along with an arms-length system of representation and an insistence that labour moves freely in response to capital movement, finally helped tip the balance of British public opinion in favour of leaving.

At the time of writing, relational instability at this macro-level continues to dog international efforts to combat Covid-19. The relative speed and success of the Covid-19 vaccine programme owes much to pre-existing business networks and a convergence of opinion among political advisers that a normally linear process should be run in parallel. More generally, the pandemic, like a war, has brought a range of players into sudden alignment on a single, well-defined and urgent issue. But despite the argument that "no one is safe until everyone is safe" the strongest alignment clearly exists between the wealthier nations. According to the *British Medical Journal* in December 2020, "At least 90 per cent of people in 67 low-income countries stand little chance of getting vaccinated against Covid-19 in 2021 because wealthy nations have reserved more than they need and developers will not share their intellectual property."[224] Four months later, WHO chief Tedros Adhanom Ghebreyesus warned that "There remains a shocking and expanding disparity in the global distribution of vaccines."[225]

In comparison, the relational underpinnings of climate change are complex. The fact that concern about it has risen significantly in many countries since 2013[226] is thanks mainly to media coverage. We can observe the shrinking icecaps and the bleaching of the Great Barrier Reef, and register that a majority in the scientific community view these as evidence of a climate catastrophe triggered, in the main, by long-term human dependence on fossil fuels.

Nevertheless, at a global scale, this step-change in mutual knowledge does not translate easily into alignment. Part of the problem, according to Yale science communication specialist Dan Kahan, is a failure to disentangle the question of "what we should do with what we know" from the question of "whose side you are on".[227] The second is about cultural identity, but has come to dominate the climate debate partly because global media does not fully bridge the gap in mutual knowledge between climate scientists and the general public, leaving some important foundations of climate science to be taken on trust – including the reliability of highly complex atmospheric modelling and what exactly will happen if targets are met or missed.

This may explain why the climate emergency can be eclipsed by more local concerns. When Pew Research surveyed attitudes to climate change in 2018, for example, 27 per cent of American Republicans said climate change was a major threat, compared with 83 per cent of Democrats – a 56 percentage point difference. Figures were below 50 per cent in both Russia and Israel.[228]

Similarly, the solution to a complex global crisis may lie in taking action at sub-global levels where human connectivity is higher. For example, according to Kahan, members of the Southeast Florida Regional Climate Compact – a coalition of local governments – have adopted a "Regional Climate Action Plan" containing over 100 distinct mitigation and adaption measures. The residents of Southeast Florida are as polarised on whether human activity is causing global warming as those in the rest of the country. But at this local scale it was far easier to disentangle questions of what science knows from questions of partisan climate politics. The deliberative process focused simply on how communities could use scientific knowledge to address the region's practical, everyday needs.[229]

Similarly, in a survey of California residents after the devastating 2020 wildfires, senior researcher at Stanford University's Bill Lane Center Iris Hui noted how "our findings show that when Republicans experience a nearby wildfire more than once, they act no differently from Democrats in their support for using public funds to subsidise adaptation measures. In other words, the partisan gap in the willingness to support climate adaptation strategies diminishes."[230]

Related to this is the desire for potentially costly sacrifices to have immediate tangible benefit. A 2019 poll conducted by the Energy Policy Institute at the University of Chicago and the Chicago-based Associated Press-NORC Center for Public Affairs Research showed that although only 44 per cent of Americans would support a carbon tax, this proportion rose to 60 per cent if the funds paid for research and development on renewable energy and to 67 per cent if the proceeds were used to restore forests, wetlands, and other environmental assets.[231]

In practice, meeting climate targets will require unpicking some of the economic mechanisms covered in this book, otherwise global financial and commodity markets will continue to incentivise behaviours at variance with priorities like preventing rainforest logging or switching to renewable energy. Given the immense and uneven costs of reducing carbon emissions, it also requires governments to agree on what kinds of timescale and load-sharing are most likely to strike the various global stakeholders as fair and achievable. Fail to do that, and alignments built around climate change may dissolve in the face of what might appear to be more immediate threats to jobs or national security.

Sample policy directions

Shocks will come. Technologies will open doors. Social outlooks will change. But the relational components of a workable society remain remarkably constant: personal and community wellbeing, the health of the body politic, and the effectiveness and sustainability of organisations, including companies (see Figure 8). It is these three imperatives that relational stability delivers because it directly addresses the terms on which human beings are connected through the mass relationships that large institutions create and define.

Figure 8. The impact of strong human connectivity for society.

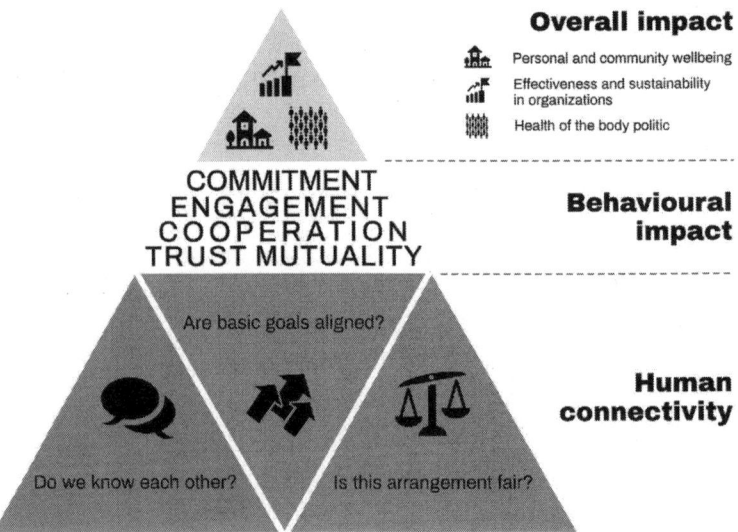

It is not within the scope of this book to set out a legislative programme, and Table 6 is meant only to indicate a few sample policy directions a government might consider in pursuit of building relational stability across the five areas covered in this chapter. The principles are simple: citizens and stakeholder groups must be able to feel familiar to one another; their core objectives must be able to align; and whatever institutional arrangements bind them together must be seen as broadly fair. In practice, this framework can function both actively (with the aim of adjusting existing rules and structures to increase human connectivity) and passively (as a standard or checklist against which other new policy proposals can be assessed).

As a political position, relational stability belongs to neither Right nor Left. It does not stand on the continuum of compromise between free enterprise and state control, but challenges the assumption beneath much Western culture that an adequate definition of human thriving can be assembled out of a kit-box of individual wealth, freedom, rights and equality. What matters, in any form of polity, is how well individuals and stakeholder groups are able to connect to one another. And that means the networks that link them together are as much part of the infrastructure as big-ticket investment items like motorways, 5G, or the national grid. Taking responsibility for those networks is the first step to a just and sustainable world. It may also be a matter of survival.

*Table 6. Suggested policy directions to promote
mutual knowledge, alignment and fairness*

COMPANIES Organise for stakeholder dialogue and benefit	<ul><li>Rebalance incentives for equity finance and debt finance</li><li>Restrain unfair advantage gained by size in competitive markets</li><li>Discourage share buybacks that damage the interests of wider stakeholders</li><li>Facilitate relational stability in company networks through an advisory body</li><li>Encourage routine engagement between companies and their stakeholders</li></ul>
POLITICS Build democratic processes that create engagement	<ul><li>Use subsidiarity as a principle of devolved government</li><li>Introduce a checklist-based relational stability impact assessment in the development of new policy proposals</li><li>Establish formal fact-checking independent of political party campaigns and require all campaign claims to carry a truth rating</li><li>Encourage engagement between potentially hostile communities</li><li>Include in the syllabus modules on the value, purpose and exercise of democracy</li><li>Promote continuity in policy objectives and key inter-institutional relationships</li></ul>

TIME	
Attribute real value to family and community networks	• Recognise the equivalent value of work and family/community involvement • Protect leisure time and increase long-term job security • Facilitate home-working and working hour flexibility • Support family formation with a view to preserving age-balance in the population • Explore metrics that allow the value of time to be measured in non-financial terms • Provide incentives for wider family groups to build financial interdependence
ECONOMY Treat labour as an associate not a cost of production	• Extend city-based or region-based economic planning • Use IT to move work to people rather than people to work • Fund local retraining in preference to exploiting cheap migrant labour • Incentivise extended family colocation as a way to build social support networks • Recast benefits and personal allowances as universal basic income
SOCIETY Prioritise human connectivity across social, institutional and media networks	• Bring human rights into a context of dialogue, reconciliation, and responsibility for third-party impact • Protect social media users by law, not anonymity • Introduce relational skill development into core school curricula • Encourage media to make major cultural and sporting events accessible to the entire national population • Introduce relational connectivity as a management principle in public sector organisations

> *"Now more than ever, as big decisions are made about our future, companies need to address environmental, social and governance risks holistically and move beyond business-as-usual."*

UN Secretary-General António Guterres, 2020[232]

9. CONCLUSION

This book is about companies, and how they can perform better if they are understood not as a nexus of stakeholders, but as a nexus of stakeholder networks.

It is also about wider society. Because what is true of companies is also true of the world at large. Modern institutions have an enormous influence on the daily lives of all of us. The vast interlocking networks in which we participate make us critically interdependent. We benefit by cooperating; the question is whether we can cooperate enough when so much of our attention is absorbed by huge impersonal networks – and specifically, since human nature is universally a mixed bag, whether the networks we create are incentivising us to cooperate or not.

Hence the core issues of Corporate Capitalism identified in this book are firstly what we call human connectivity in organisational networks and secondly the need to realign corporate stakeholder relationship priorities.

People are adept at forming relationships, finding common cause, and sharing effort and reward. The problems come with numbers. When members of a network no longer know one another, when stakeholder groups have divergent goals, and when arrangements are fairer for some than for others, these relational instabilities are apt to make cooperation difficult.

Difficult – but not impossible. Even complex global relationships, like the ones that drive climate change or the AI-driven arms race, ultimately work by the same rules. Understand the networks, build human connectivity, and you have the beginnings of a solution.

In this sense, business represents a logical place to start. Companies are, to a large extent, independent fiefdoms in which some of the rules by which stakeholders connect can be rewritten. The central part of this book explores ten ways a board of directors can achieve this to make a company network more relationally stable. A similar approach could be taken with public sector organisations or government.

Not to be proactive in this – in effect to take human connectivity for granted – creates risk. Negatively, in the sense that it limits the power of institutions to cooperate in tackling shared threats. Positively, in that mutual knowledge, alignment and fairness may be worn so thin that the institutions themselves lose legitimacy when shocks occur, and are eventually overwhelmed. Hints of this were evident in the fractious transition of power in the 2020 US presidential election.[233]

Perhaps the most pressing reason for building human connectivity is that there are other ways of organising society. The purposive expansion of machine learning, facial recognition and surveillance in China offers a glimpse of an alternative future: one where states achieve a version of social harmony without reference to the human soul. In the end, therefore,

tackling the issue of human connectivity in networks and the realignment of stakeholder relationship priorities in organisations is about more than making Corporate Capitalism acceptable to society. It is about asking ourselves what kind of world we want to live in.

WHERE NEXT?

Each of us, personally and through the organisations in which we work, can build human connectivity. This includes the choices we make as to which relationships to enter into, the conduct of those relationships, and the ways in which we shape the opportunities for connectivity for others. Building connectivity is helped by developing a better understanding of the current state of the relationships to which we are party, or perhaps could or should be. It involves strengthening relational capability, reviewing the purpose of organisations, understanding the impact of our choices and actions, learning from others, and reforming the systems that shape our choices and opportunities. There is no one-time solution but rather a constant process of creation and re-creation where both action and inaction shape relationships.

As the case studies in this book illustrate, recognition of the importance of relationships is widespread. There is a wealth of insight and experience to be found in different countries and sectors, some focused on specific relational challenges and skills, and others addressing wider systemic issues. It is far beyond the scope of any one organisation to map all the insights, resources, tools or initiatives that might inform connectivity. Nevertheless, starting points are essential and the three questions at the heart of this book – how well people or organisations know each other, whether goals are aligned, and whether arrangements are fair – provide a useful rule of thumb.

More accurate mapping of networks, and more nuanced insight into specific relationships, are both preconditions for enabling dialogue and having a better understanding of how connectivity might be strengthened, as well as the risks of failing to do so.

It is essential data that makes relationships more tangible. Consultants, trainers and advisers can also enable access to the wealth of available relational insight, facilitate difficult conversations, and develop both individual and organisational capability in building and sustaining connectivity.

The Relationships Foundation (www.relationships foundation.org), which has co-sponsored this book, has developed tools and partnerships over the years to connect people who want to implement this in their organisations. Details can be found through a link on its homepage. It offers a number of ways to begin – from self-assessment tools through to measurement dashboards and advisory services through its partners in different countries around the world.

A core message of this book has also been that our actions and opportunities are shaped by the systems in which we operate. Reforming them requires both political and cultural change and thus a wide coalition. Our experience over many years has been that despite the many initiatives and the depth of latent concern for relationships, other short-term priorities and pressures too often come to dominate. Deep-rooted systemic reform is an endeavour which requires patience. Encouragement and learning are found through connection with others on the same journey. The work of Relationships Foundation and its partners will continue to promote practitioners and initiatives that can be part of this reform process. You can connect with others through connecting with the Foundation.

The best place to start is with the relationships closest to you: your board, your team, your customers or suppliers, and your community. It is here that joy, justice and prosperity can be found, and secured for others.

> *"The purpose of a business is to make a profit so that the business can do something more or better. That 'something' becomes the real justification for the business."*

CHARLES HANDY, 2002[234]

APPENDIX 1:
REPORTING AND
METRICS

Organisational networks have multiple stakeholder groups and a finite number of crucial (performance-sensitive) stakeholder interfaces. The latter are both internal (including management/employees, board/management, subsidiary/subsidiary, parent company/subsidiary) and external (including company/supplier, company/customer, company/shareholders, company/regulators). A company's map of its stakeholder networks for its products and services should therefore be actively and systematically reviewed and its assumptions tested to ensure that the most important relationships which are key to a company's performance and productivity are given priority for examination.

Assessing compliance requires accurate measurement. Evidence-based examination of a corporation's relational stability would be a regular requirement in annual reports, outlining how the company – both in policy and practice – recognises stakeholder needs and contributions, measures human connectivity between its stakeholder groups, and addresses particular areas of relational instability through dialogue and adjusted procedures.

The first stage, in respect of any given interface of the network, is to identify what rules, procedures, schedules, conditions, and protocols bear upon the parties, and how these are affecting human connectivity. The second is to engage in a bilateral analysis of the way the relationships inside the structure actually work. The bilateral requirement is crucial because fairness and perception have to be assessed from both sides – something that customer satisfaction surveys and employee attitude surveys cannot do. Also, steps must be taken, and be seen to be taken, to ensure that more vulnerable parties (employees and suppliers, for example) do not feel under pressure to provide answers that they think directors want to hear. The Relational Stability Agency would work with companies to identify a suitable and straightforward metric.

For purposes of comparison between organisations, and within and between nations, it is useful to adopt a standard conceptual foundation to assess relationship quality. A strong contender is Relational Analytics, which uses a framework (Relational Proximity®) that expands the three-questions approach used in this book, measuring human connectivity across the dimensions of communication, time, information, power and purpose. As such it quantifies not only attitudes and behaviours but the potential of the relationship, as defined and practised, to support the social qualities that are likely to benefit both the parties and the organisation as a whole.[235]

APPENDIX 2: THE RELATIONAL STABILITY STRATEGY FOR BUSINESS

1. Redefine the purpose of the company and make it known to investors, directors and employees
2. Promote dialogue among all significant stakeholder groups, using live meetings and digital platforms
3. Work towards having a significant proportion of the shares owned by employees, individuals or family trusts
4. Work towards having a high proportion of shares owned on a long-term basis
5. Ensure that management has respect for the interests of employees
6. Minimise remuneration differentials within the business
7. Treat suppliers fairly by paying them promptly and giving them support to develop their businesses
8. Treat customers and the local community fairly

9. Minimise the risk of financial instability to protect the company and its stakeholders

10. Fulfil obligations to wider society

SELECTED
BIBLIOGRAPHY

Ashcroft, J, R Childs, A Myers, and M Schluter, *The Relational Lens: Understanding, Measuring and Managing Stakeholder Relationships*, Cambridge University Press, 2017.

Asen, E and D Binn, "What European OECD Countries Are Doing about Digital Services Taxes", *Tax Foundation*, 25 March 2021.

Calderone, G, *Bloomberg – Are You a Robot?*, Bloomberg, 27 January 2019.

Department for Business, Energy and Industrial Strategy, UK Policy White Paper, "Restoring trust in audit and corporate governance", March 2021.

Financial Reporting Council, "Review of Corporate Governance Reporting", November 2020.

Flammer, C, M W Toffel, and K Viswanathan. "Shareholder Activism and Firms' Voluntary Disclosure of Climate Change Risk", *Harvard Business School*, 2019.

Goyder, G, *The Just Enterprise, A Blueprint for the Responsible Company*, Adamantine Press, 1993.

Haldane, A, "Who Owns a Company?", Talk presented at the University of Edinburgh Corporate Finance Conference, 28 July 2015.

Handy, C, "What's a business for?", *Harvard Business Review*, December 2002.

Handy, C, *The Empty Raincoat: Making sense of the future*, Arrow Books, 2011.

Keynes, J M, "National Self-Sufficiency", *The Yale Review*, Vol. 22, No. 4 (1933).

Kustin, B, "Insights into responsible business", part of the Oxford Ownership Project, Saïd Business School.

Lazonick, W, M E Sakinç and M Hopkins, "Why Stock Buybacks Are Dangerous for the Economy", *Harvard Business Review*, January, 2020.

Liker, J, *The Toyota Way: 14 Management Principles from the World's Greatest Manufacturer*. McGraw-Hill, 2004.

Mayer, C P, *Firm Commitment: Why the Corporation Is Failing Us and How to Restore Trust in It*, Oxford University Press, 2013.

Modigliani, F and M H Miller. "The Cost of Capital, Corporation Finance and the Theory of Investment", *The American Economic Review* 48, no. 3 (1958): 261–97.

Narayanan, V G, "How to Fix Executive Pay", *Harvard Business Review*, June 2009.

Palladino, L, "Examining Corporate Priorities: The Impact of Stock Buybacks on Workers, Communities and Investors", The Harvard Law School Forum on Corporate Governance, 22 October 2019.

Pettifor, A, *The Production of Money: How to Break the Power of Bankers*, London: Verso, 2018.

Rushworth, J and M Schluter, *Transforming Capitalism from Within: A Relational Approach to the Purpose, Performance and Assessment of Companies*, Relational Research and Relationships Foundation, Cambridge, 2013.

Rushworth, J and A Reisberg, "Transforming Capitalism from Within: A Relational Approach to Company Management and Operations", *International Corporate Rescue Special Issue*, Chase Cambria, 2014.

Schluter, M and D J Lee, *The R Factor*, Hodder and Stoughton, 1993.

Stout, L A, "On the Rise of Shareholder Primacy, Signs of Its Fall, and the Return of Managerialism (in the Closet)", 2013. *Cornell Law Faculty Publications*, Paper 865.

The British Academy, "Principles for Purposeful Business", The British Academy, 2019.

ENDNOTES

[1] Wikipedia defines State Capitalism as an economic system in which the state undertakes business and commercial (i.e. for-profit) economic activity and where the means of production are nationalised as state-owned enterprises (including the processes of capital accumulation, centralised management and wage labour), https://en.wikipedia.org/wiki/State_capitalism

[2] Development Initiatives, Poverty trends: global, regional and national, Factsheet, 10 November 2021, https://devinit.org/resources/poverty-trends-global-regional-and-national/

[3] The message was stark. Companies, he said, should make a positive contribution to society – and not just deliver profits to shareholders – or they would risk losing the support of his $1.7 trillion fund. https://sustainiaworld.com/blackrock-ceo-larry-fink-letter-to-ceos-words-or-action/.

[4] Adam Lashinsky, "An Insider Takes Aim at Corporate America's 'Elite Charade,'" *Fortune*, September 20, 2019. https://fortune.com/longform/anand-giridharadas-winners-take-all.

[5] Recent figures show that the world's 10 largest companies paid a record total of $1.37 trillion in dividends in 2018, equivalent to the gross domestic product of medium-sized economies such as Mexico or Australia.

[6] Colin P Mayer, *Firm Commitment: Why the Corporation Is Failing Us and How to Restore Trust in It* (Oxford Univ. Press, 2013).

[7] R Edward Freeman, "Stakeholder Management and Reputation" in Values and Ethics for the 21st Century. https://www.bbvaopenmind.com/wp-content/uploads/2013/02/Stakeholder-Management-and-Reputation_R.Edward-Freeman.pdf.

[8] Oliver Milman, "Deepwater Horizon Disaster Altered Building Blocks of Ocean Life," *The Guardian*, 28 June 2018). https://www.theguardian.com/environment/2018/jun/28/bp-deepwater-horizon-oil-spill-report.

[9] Bill Chappell. "'It Was Installed for This Purpose,' VW's U.S. CEO Tells Congress about Defeat Device." NPR, 8 October 2015. https://www.npr.org/sections/thetwo-way/2015/10/08/446861855/volkswagen-u-s-ceo-faces-questions-on-capitol-hill.

[10] The ideas behind relational stability were first laid out by Michael Schluter and David Lee in *The R Factor* (Hodder and Stoughton, 1993), and further expanded in John Ashcroft's *The Relational Lens: Understanding, Measuring and Managing Stakeholder Relationships.* (Cambridge, United Kingdom: Cambridge University Press, 2017). For more, see also: Jonathan Rushworth and Michael Schluter, "Transforming Capitalism from Within: a Relational Approach to the Purpose, Performance and Assessment of Companies" (Relationships Foundation and Relational Research, 2011) and Jonathan Rushworth and Dr Arad Reisberg, formerly of University College London, now Professor of Corporate Law and Finance, Head of Brunel Law School, Brunel University, London, "Transforming Capitalism from Within: A Relational Approach to Company Management and Operations," (International Corporate Rescue, Chase Cambria,

2014). http://www.chasecambria.com/site/journal/special/issue.
php?id=134.

[11] Note, however, that at an individual level it becomes harder to
distinguish network rules from behaviours. We all understand
human connectivity and use it instinctively to regulate our
interaction with others: meeting more or less often, seeking
common ground, treating people with politeness and respect.
Also, its three elements are routinely invoked in political
discourse to justify stances on issues ranging from immigration
to vaccine rollouts.

[12] In general, this is because in a small, informal network (a
reading group, a local pub, a running club), members will have
a high degree of control over human connectivity and navigate
it almost instinctively. They join through shared interest, deal
directly with others at a chosen level of participation, and can
withdraw if they feel their voice is not heard. In larger networks,
human connectivity is more likely to be controlled centrally
and to be constrained by the needs, objectives and geographical
spread of the organisation.

[13] The Editors of Encyclopedia Britannica. "Peasants' Revolt |
English History." In Encyclopædia Britannica. Accessed 17 June
2021. https://www.britannica.com/event/Peasants-Revolt.

[14] Jeff Desjardins. "How Much Data Is Generated Each Day?"
World Economic Forum, April 17, 2019. https://www.weforum.
org/agenda/2019/04/how-much-data-is-generated-each-day-
cf4bddf29f.

[15] Sankalp Phartiyal and Neha Dasgupta. "India Widens Internet
Shutdown to Parts of Delhi to Curb Protests." Reuters, 20
December 2019. https://www.reuters.com/article/us-india-
citizenship-mobile-services-idUSKBN1YN0MX.

[16] Elizabeth Economy. "The Great Firewall of China: Xi Jinping's
Internet Shutdown." The Guardian, 29 June 2018. https://www.
theguardian.com/news/2018/jun/29/the-great-firewall-of-china-
xi-jinpings-internet-shutdown.

[17] For example, the Pfizer vaccine for Covid-19 requires 280 inputs from suppliers in 19 countries – meaning that vaccine production is difficult to replicate in poorer countries.

[18] "Total Market Value of U.S. Stock Market." Siblis Research. Accessed June 25, 2021. https://siblisresearch.com/data/us-stock-market-value/.

[19] Andrew G. Haldane, "Who owns a company?" Speech at the University of Edinburgh Corporate Finance Conference, Edinburgh, 22 May 2015. https://www.bankofengland.co.uk/speech/2015/who-owns-a-company.

[20] Andrew G. Haldane, "Who owns a company?" Speech at the University of Edinburgh Corporate Finance Conference, Edinburgh, 22 May 2015. https://www.bankofengland.co.uk/speech/2015/who-owns-a-company.

[21] *New York Times*, 14 January 1922.

[22] Jeff, Cruttenden. "For the Price of One Share of Stock, You Could Influence a Billion-Dollar Company." Entrepreneur, 23 October 2018. https://www.entrepreneur.com/article/320778.

[23] In high-frequency trading (HFT), for instance, transactions are made by algorithms run on high-speed computers capable of placing millions of orders each day and gaining advantage through moving milliseconds before the competition to achieve profit on wafer thin margins. The US has always been the main hub for HFT, which has accounted for at least half of all the volume within the US equity market every single year since 2008. But revenue in 2017 was around 86 per cent lower than it was when HFT was at its peak in 2009. In eight years high-frequency traders in the US have seen revenue from the equity markets collapse from a peak of $7.2 billion to below $1 billion in 2017 for the first time since the financial crash, according to estimates from consultancy firm TABB Group. The problem is that the competitive advantage for high-frequency traders all but disappears once the technology is widely available and co-location charges – shortening the distance between HFT computers and servers – go up.

[24] Gabriel T. Rubin. "Show Us Your Climate Risks, Investors Tell Companies." *Wall Street Journal*, 28 February 2019. https://www.wsj.com/articles/show-us-your-climate-risks-investors-tell-companies-11551349800.

[25] Caroline Flammer, Michael Toffel, and Kala Viswanathan. "Shareholder Activism and Firms' Voluntary Disclosure of Climate Change Risk." Harvard Business School, 2019. https://www.hbs.edu/ris/Publication%20Files/20-049_90d4fcb5-4d13-4ebe-92e9-8d0f086785b8.pdf.

[26] Blake Morgan. "101 Companies Committed to Reducing Their Carbon Footprint." Forbes, 26 August 2019. https://www.forbes.com/sites/blakemorgan/2019/08/26/101-companies-committed-to-reducing-their-carbon-footprint.

[27] Jeffrey K. Liker, *The Toyota Way : 14 Management Principles from the World's Greatest Manufacturer.* McGraw-Hill, 2004.

[28] "Supplier Relations." Toyotauk.com. Accessed 25 June 2021. https://www.toyotauk.com/toyota-in-the-uk/supplier-relations.html.

[29] Robert E. Cole, "What Really Happened to Toyota?" MIT Sloan Management Review, 22 June 2011. https://sloanreview.mit.edu/article/what-really-happened-to-toyota/.

[30] A.A. Berle and G.C. Means, *The Modern Corporation and Private Property* (2nd edn., Harcourt, Brace and World, New York, 1967).

[31] Lynn A. Stout, "On the Rise of Shareholder Primacy, Signs of Its Fall, and the Return of Managerialism (in the Closet)" (2013). Cornell Law Faculty Publications. Paper 865, p.1171. http://scholarship.law.cornell.edu/facpub/865.

[32] Shareholders only own an interest in a company's profitability. They have no right to the proceeds of the sale of corporate assets, and, if the company is liquidated, the banks and other creditors will rank ahead of them to claim whatever remains.

33 Lynn A. Stout, "On the Rise of Shareholder Primacy, Signs of Its Fall, and the Return of Managerialism (in the Closet)" (2013). Cornell Law Faculty Publications. Paper 865, p.1171. http:// scholarship.law.cornell.edu/facpub/865.

34 S.172 (1) Companies Act 2006 provides that a director of a company must act in the way he considers, in good faith, would be most likely to promote the success of the company for the benefit of its members as a whole, and in doing so have regard (amongst other matters) to: the likely consequences of any decision in the long term, the interests of the company's employees, the need to foster the company's business relationships with suppliers, customers and others, the impact of the company's operations on the community and the environment, the desirability of the company maintaining a reputation for high standards of business conduct, and the need to act fairly as between members of the company. It should be noted that s172(2) provides (in summary) that where the purposes of the company consist of or include purposes other than the benefit of its members, the directors must promote the success of the company to achieve those purposes. This could apply, for instance to a charity, but could also apply to any company seeking to benefit others rather than its shareholders (members). See https://www.legislation. gov.uk/ukpga/2006/46/part/10/chapter/2/enacted/data.xht

35 S.168 Companies Act 2006.

36 John Maynard Keynes, "National Self-Sufficiency" *The Yale Review*, Vol. 22, No. 4 (1933), pp. 755–769. https://www. mtholyoke.edu/acad/intrel/interwar/keynes.htm.

37 Guerrera, Francesco, "Welch Condemns Share Price Focus," *Financial Times*. Accessed August 2011. http://www. ft.com/intl/cms/s/0/294ff1f2-0f27-11de-ba10-0000779fd2ac. html#axzz1WWQxsecY.

38 "Toshiba Ex-CEOs Unlikely to Face Charges over Scandal: Source." Reuters, 8 July 2016. https://www.reuters.com/article/us-toshiba-scandal-idUSKCN0ZO1AB.

[39] Patrick Worrall. "FactCheck: Why Does Amazon Pay so Little Tax?" Channel 4 News, 3 August 2018. https://www.channel4. com/news/factcheck/factcheck-why-does-amazon-pay-so-little-tax.

[40] Ashley Armstrong. "Amazon Pays Just £220m Tax on British Revenue of £10.9bn." The Times, 4 September 2019. https://www. thetimes.co.uk/article/amazon-pays-just-220m-tax-on-british-earnings-of-10-9bn-vv9fwxx52. Of course, this takes no account of the amount of indirect taxes paid by Amazon, which are also paid by every company operating in the UK.

[41] "G7: Rich nations back deal to tax multinationals", BBC, 5 June 2021. https://www.bbc.co.uk/news/world-57368247.

[42] Negotiated by the Organisation for Economic Co-operation and Development, reported in The Times on 9 October 2021.

[43] Mark Carney, "Inclusive Capitalism: Creating a Sense of the Systemic," Bank of England, May 27, 2014. https://www. bankofengland.co.uk/speech/2014/inclusive-capitalism-creating-a-sense-of-the-systemic.

[44] Andy Verity. "Banks under Fire for Coronavirus Loan Tactics." BBC, 30 March 2020. https://www.bbc.co.uk/news/business-52043896.

[45] In 2009, Kraft Foods Inc. obtained US$9 billion in bridge financing from a group of nine banks to back its £10.2 billion bid for Britain's Cadbury Plc.

[46] S. Çelik, Demirtaş and M. Isaksson. "Corporate Bond Markets in a Time of Unconventional Monetary Policy", OECD Capital Market Series, Paris, 2019. https://www.oecd.org/corporate/ corporate-bond-markets-in-a-time-of-unconventional-monetary-policy.htm.

[47] "US Budget Deficit Soars to $3tn Record." BBC News, 11 September 2020. https://www.bbc.co.uk/news/business-54126226.

[48] Annie Lowrey. "Millennials Don't Stand a Chance." *The Atlantic*, 13 April 2020, https://www.theatlantic.com/ideas/archive/2020/04/millennials-are-new-lost-generation/609832/.

[49] Ben Chapman. "Majority of the World's Richest Entities Are Corporations, Not Governments." *The Independent*, 17 October 2018. https://www.independent.co.uk/news/business/news/companies-bigger-governments-un-human-rights-council-meeting-a8588676.html.

[50] "Fortune Global 500 List 2018: See Who Made It." Fortune. Accessed 26 June 2021. http://fortune.com/global500/.

[51] An investigation by the FCA found that between 2008 and 2013 GRG had focused on extracting money from thousands of companies, with many business owners handled by the unit claiming that RBS ruined their livelihoods. The GRG division handled small and medium companies in financial difficulties, with a view to their being restructured or to manage the cessation of their business. The main focus after the financial crisis of 2008 seemed to be to liquidate companies rather than support them, often when they were financially viable.

[52] According to the Federation of Small Businesses. Quoted by Lauren Hellicar, "50,000 small businesses fold due to late payments each year", 13 May 2019. https://www.simplybusiness.co.uk/knowledge/articles/2019/05/50000-small-businesses-fail-due-to-late-payments/.

[53] Eoin Burke-Kennedy. "Multinationals channelled €27bn through Ireland in 2016, report claims", 1 July 2021. https://www.irishtimes.com/business/economy/multinationals-channelled-27bn-through-ireland-in-2016-report-claims-1.4608186.

[54] Joe Pinsker. "The Covert World of People Trying to Edit Wikipedia—for Pay." *The Atlantic*, August 11, 2015. https://www.theatlantic.com/business/archive/2015/08/wikipedia-editors-for-pay/393926/.

[55] https://www.bizjournals.com/sanjose/news/2019/04/01/zuckerberg-s-call-to-regulate-facebook-explained.html.

[56] Kelvin Chan, "EU, Britain to toughen rules, fines for tech giants," Associated Press, 15 December 2020, https://apnews. com/article/business-media-bills-social-media-19038a8f0a6844 8ce6037308930a5efc

[57] Hakanen, Jari J., Annina Ropponen, Wilmar B. Schaufeli, and Hans De Witte. "Who Is Engaged at Work?" *Journal of Occupational & Environmental Medicine* 61, no. 5 (May 2019): 373–81. https://doi.org/10.1097/jom.0000000000001528.

[58] Jo Faragher. "FTSE 100 CEOs Earn Average Annual Wage in Just 34 Hours," Personnel Today, 6 January 2021. https://www. personneltoday.com/hr/ftse-100-ceos-earn-average-annual-wage-in-just-34-hours/.

[59] According to figures from the Economic Policy Institute. See https://www.cbsnews.com/news/ceo-pay-in-940-more-than-40-years-ago-workers-make-12-more/.

[60] Alexia Fernández Campbell. "CEOs Made 287 Times More Money than Their Workers in 2018." Vox. Vox, 26 June 2019. https://www.vox.com/policy-and-politics/2019/6/26/18744304/ceo-pay-ratio-disclosure-2018.

[61] Diana Hembree, "CEO Pay Skyrockets To 361 Times That Of The Average Worker", 22 May 2018. https://www.forbes.com/sites/dianahembree/2018/05/22/ceo-pay-skyrockets-to-361-times-that-of-the-average-worker/. Deloitte LLP and the High Pay Centre publish information each year on executive remuneration for listed UK companies. According to the High Pay Centre, in 2020 the median FTSE 100 CEO was paid £2.69m, 86 times the median full-time employee in the UK. This was a fall from the median CEO pay of £3.25m in 2019. The CEO of AstraZeneca was reported to be the highest paid in 2020, earning £15.45m and the CEO of Experian £10.3m.

[62] https://www.ft.com/content/199fbd0c-7cc0-4af0-b1a0-a4286fdd1280

[63] Note that a contrasting problem occurs when regulation is confined to a local level. In March 2016, the European Parliament

published an independent study that revealed corruption accounted for almost €1 trillion euros – 14 per cent of the entire GDP of the EU. For the most part, the problem lies with ties between the political class and industry at national level and particularly in the east and south of the EU. The report concluded: "Corruption is associated with more unequal societies, higher levels of organised crime, weaker rule of law, reduced voter turnout in national parliamentary elections and lower trust in EU institutions." See: http://www.rand.org/randeurope/research/projects/corruption-costs-of-non-europe.

[64] Steve Goldstein. "Here's the Staggering Amount Banks Have Been Fined since the Financial Crisis." MarketWatch, 24 February 2018. https://www.marketwatch.com/story/banks-have-been-fined-a-staggering-243-billion-since-the-financial-crisis-2018-02-20.

[65] Jessica Davies, "Guide to European Regulators' War with the Tech Platforms." Digiday, 8 July 2019. https://digiday.com/media/guide-european-regulators-war-tech-platforms/.

[66] Luzi Hail, Ahmed Tahoun, and Clare Wang. "How Well Does Financial Regulation Work?" Institute for New Economic Thinking, 15 March 2018. https://www.ineteconomics.org/perspectives/blog/how-well-does-financial-reg-work.

[67] Tim Koller, James Manyika, and Sree Ramaswamy. "The Case against Corporate Short Termism | McKinsey." McKinsey, 4 August 2017. https://www.mckinsey.com/mgi/overview/in-the-news/the-case-against-corporate-short-termism#.

[68] Rachelle C. Sampson, and Yuan Shi. "Are US Firms Becoming More Short-Term Oriented? Evidence of Shifting Firm Time Horizons from Implied Discount Rates, 1980–2013." SSRN, 13 September 2016. https://ssrn.com/abstract=2837524.

[69] The UK Government is now considering funding this research, as pharmaceutical companies are reluctant to carry out long-term research where a financial return is uncertain.

[70] Koller, Manyika, and Ramaswamy. "The Case against Corporate Short Termism | McKinsey." McKinsey, 4 August 2017. https://www.mckinsey.com/mgi/overview/in-the-news/the-case-against-corporate-short-termism#.

[71] "UK CEOs Have Less Time than Ever to Make Their Mark." PwC, 15 May 2017. https://www.pwc.co.uk/press-room/press-releases/uk-ceos-have-less-time-than-ever-to-make-an-impact.html.

[72] John Browne and Robin Nuttall. "Beyond Corporate Social Responsibility: Integrated External Engagement," McKinsey & Company, 1 March 2013. https://www.mckinsey.com/business-functions/strategy-and-corporate-finance/our-insights/beyond-corporate-social-responsibility-integrated-external-engagement.

[73] S.172 (2) Companies Act 2006.

[74] "Business Roundtable Redefines the Purpose of a Corporation to Promote 'An Economy That Serves All Americans'", 19 August 2019. https://www.businessroundtable.org/business-roundtable-redefines-the-purpose-of-a-corporation-to-promote-an-economy-that-serves-all-americans.

[75] Jasper Jolly. "Investing in Firms with Better Record on Social Issues Pays, Study Finds." The Guardian, 18 May 2020. https://www.theguardian.com/business/2020/may/18/investing-in-firms-with-better-record-on-social-issues-pays-study-finds.

[76] "Gallup Employee Engagement Center." Gallup.com. Accessed 26 June 2021. https://q12.gallup.com/Public/en-us/Features.

[77] Jeffrey Liker, *The Toyota Way: 14 Management Principles from the World's Greatest Manufacturer*. McGraw-Hill, 2004. p.202.

[78] Peter Strozniak. "Toyota Alters Face of Production." Industry Week, 21 December 2004. https://www.industryweek.com/operations/continuous-improvement/article/21947002/toyota-alters-face-of-production.

[79] "Our Purpose." Amerisourcebergen.com, 2021. https://www.amerisourcebergen.com/about-us/our-purpose.

[80] Justin Young, "Unilever's Vision Statement & Mission Statement (An Analysis)," 21 February 2017. http://panmore.com/unilever-vision-statement-mission-statement-analysis

[81] "Philosophy | Corporate | CASIO." CASIO Official Website. Accessed 26 June 2021. https://world.casio.com/corporate/principle/.

[82] Andrea Garnero, "What We Do and Don't Know About Worker Representation on Boards", *Harvard Business Review*, 6 September 2018. https://hbr.org/2018/09/what-we-do-and-dont-know-about-worker-representation-on-boards.

[83] "Integrated Reporting." integratedreporting.org. Accessed 26 June 2021. http://integratedreporting.org.

[84] "BAE Systems Trade Union Network Builds Strategy." IndustriALL, 28 November 2016. http://www.industriall-union.org/bae-systems-trade-union-network-builds-strategy.

[85] Nadine Hack. "How Deeply Engaging Stakeholders Changes Everything." Forbes, 3 May 2011. https://www.forbes.com/sites/85broads/2011/05/03/how-deeply-engaging-stakeholders-changes-everything/#4905026d6932.

[86] "IR Calendar | IR Activities | IR | Company – Hyundai Worldwide." HYUNDAI MOTORS. Accessed 26 June 2021. https://www.hyundai.com/worldwide/en/company/ir/ir-activities/ir-calendar.

[87] "2020 Annual Report." L'Oréal Finance. Accessed 26 June 2021. https://www.loreal-finance.com/eng/annual-report.

[88] "Ethics Correspondents, the Everyday Ambassadors." L'Oréal Finance: Annual Report 2018. Accessed 26 June 2021. https://www.loreal-finance.com/en/annual-report-2018/ethics-1-4/ethics-correspondents-everyday-ambassadors-1-4-1/.

[89] Hack, "How Deeply Engaging Stakeholders Changes Everything." Forbes, 3 May 2011. https://www.forbes.com/sites/85broads/2011/05/03/how-deeply-engaging-stakeholders-changes-everything/#4905026d6932.

[90] "Packaging & Waste." corporate.mcdonalds.com. Accessed 26 June 2021. https://corporate.mcdonalds.com/corpmcd/our-purpose-and-impact/our-planet/packaging-and-waste.html.

[91] https://corporate.mcdonalds.com/corpmcd/our-purpose-and-impact/our-planet/packaging-and-waste.html

[92] "Hitachi Investor Day : Investor Relations : Hitachi Global." www.hitachi.com. Accessed 26 June 2021. http://www.hitachi.com/IR-e/library/irday/index.html.

[93] "Opinions | KEPCO -." home.kepco.co.kr. Accessed 26 June 2021. http://home.kepco.co.kr/kepco/EN/que/EnQueDispView.do?menuCd=EN040107.

[94] "Integrated Reports | IR Materials | Investor Relations | FUJIFILM Holdings." ir.fujifilm.com. Accessed 26 June 2021. https://ir.fujifilm.com/en/investors/ir-materials/integrated-report.html.

[95] Yoshihiro Hidaka. "Top Message – Company Information." Yamaha. Accessed 26 June 2021. https://global.yamaha-motor.com/about/csr/message/.

[96] "The Anatomy of a Hackathon: A 24-Hour Infographic." The Shutterstock Blog, 21 July 2014. https://www.shutterstock.com/blog/hackathon-infographic-shutterstock.

[97] Reported in *The Times,* 8 October 2021.

[98] This is set out in greater detail in Jonathan Rushworth and Michael Schluter, "Transforming Capitalism from Within, Relational Research and Relationships Foundation", Cambridge, 2013, p.15.

[99] TTP Group plc Report and Accounts 2020, p.5.

[100] Aime Williams, "Why big companies are listening to small shareholders. Now is the time for private investors to stand up and be counted," *Financial Times*, 25 August 2017.

[101] Rueil Malmaison, "VINCI's 100,000 employees in France become Group shareholders", 6 February 2020. https://www.globenewswire.com/news-release/2020/02/06/1981327/0/en/VINCI-s-100-000-employees-in-France-become-Group-shareholders.html

[102] Karishma Vaswani. "Huawei: The World's Most Controversial Company", BBC, 6 March 2019. https://www.bbc.co.uk/news/resources/idt-sh/Huawei. See also: https://www.huawei.com/uk/press-events/annual-report/2019.

[103] "The Ownership Dividend: The Economic Case for Employee Ownership", June 2018. https://employeeownership.co.uk/wp-content/uploads/The_Ownership_Dividend_The_economic_case_for_employee_ownership.pdf. See also: https://www.unilever.com/about/who-we-are/about-Unilever/ and https://www.symology.co.uk/Products.

[104] "Compensation." www.bouygues.com. Accessed 26 June 2021. https://www.bouygues.com/en/talent/your-career-at-bouygues/compensation-and-employee-share-ownership/.

[105] Patrick Bolton and Frédéric Samama. "Loyalty-Shares: Rewarding Long-Term Investors." SSRN, 2013. https://ssrn.com/abstract=2371482.

[106] Andy Haldane. "Who Owns a Company?", presented at the University of Edinburgh Corporate Finance Conference, 28 July 2015. https://www.bankofengland.co.uk/speech/2015/who-owns-a-company.

[107] "Shareholders." Air Liquide. Accessed 25 April 2019. https://www.airliquide.com/shareholders.

[108] "A Long-Term Investment." Air Liquide. Accessed 26 June 2021. https://www.airliquide.com/investors/long-term-investment.

[109] "A principles-based approach", LTSE. Accessed 26 June 2021. https://longtermstockexchange.com/listings/principles/.

[110] "Long Working Hours Killing 745,000 People a Year, Study Finds." BBC News, 17 May 2021. https://www.bbc.co.uk/news/business-57139434.

[111] "Long Working Hours Killing 745,000 People a Year, Study Finds." BBC News, 17 May 2021. https://www.bbc.co.uk/news/business-57139434. See also: "The Link between Job Satisfaction and Firm Value, with Implications for Corporate Social Responsibility." *Academy of Management Perspectives* 26, no. 4 (November 2012): 1–19. https://doi.org/10.5465/amp.2012.0046.

[112] "Four-day week 'an overwhelming success' in Iceland", BBC News, 6 July 2021. https://www.bbc.co.uk/news/business-57724779.

[113] "Quorum Network Resources Ltd," 8 May 2018. https://scottishbusinesspledge.scot/case_studies/quorum-network-resources-ltd/.

[114] "Employee Ownership Association." Employee Ownership Association. Accessed 26 June 2021. https://employeeownership.co.uk/what-is-employee-ownership/. See also: "John Lewis Partnership – Employee Ownership." Johnlewispartnership.co.uk. Accessed 26 June 2021. https://www.johnlewispartnership.co.uk/work/employee-ownership.html.

[115] "With No Certainty over Retail's Future, Are John Lewis Staff Now Being Undersold?" *The Guardian,* March 14, 2021. https://www.theguardian.com/business/2021/mar/14/with-no-certainty-over-retails-future-are-john-lewis-staff-now-being-undersold.

[116] Zoe Wood. "Richer Sounds Founder Hands over Control of Hi-Fi and TV Firm to Staff." *The Guardian*, 14 May 2019. https://www.theguardian.com/business/2019/may/14/richer-sounds-staff-julian-richer.

[117] "Ministry of Fun | Admiral Group Plc." admiralgroup.co.uk. Accessed 27 June 2021. https://admiralgroup.co.uk/our-culture/ministry-fun.

[118] Zoe Thomas, "Best Big Company to Work for 2019: Fun and Profits at Admiral," *The Times*, 24 February 2019, sec. Best Companies to Work For 2019. https://www.thetimes.co.uk/article/sunday-times-best-big-companies-to-work-for-2019-admiral-6chfq9cv9.

[119] "HubSpot Careers | Benefits." www.hubspot.com. Accessed 27 June 2021. https://www.hubspot.com/careers/benefits.

[120] "Our People." Aviva.com. Accessed 27 June 2021. https://www.aviva.com/about-us/our-people/.

[121] Netflix. "Work Life Philosophy." Netflix.com. Accessed 27 June 2021. https://jobs.netflix.com/work-life-philosophy. See also: "Inclusion & Diversity." Netflix.com. Accessed 27 Jun 2021. https://jobs.netflix.com/diversity.

[122] "Canon's Approach." Accessed 27 June 2021. https://global.canon/en/csr/report/pdf/canon-sus-2019-e-20.pdf.

[123] "FTSE 100 CEOs Earn Average £900 an Hour | Accountancy Daily." www.accountancydaily.co. Accessed 27 June 2021. https://www.accountancydaily.co/ftse-100-ceos-earn-average-ps900-hour.

[124] V.G. Narayanan, "How to Fix Executive Pay", *Harvard Business Review*, 17 June 2009.

[125] Chad Bray. "British Regulator Proposes Additional Rules to Claw Back Banker Bonuses." *The New York Times*, 14 January 2016, sec. Business. https://www.nytimes.com/2016/01/14/business/dealbook/britain-banker-bonus-rules.html.

[126] UK Policy White Paper published on 18 March 2021 by Department for Business, Energy and Industrial Strategy, entitled "Restoring trust in audit and corporate governance", which sets out proposals for consultation to strengthen the UK's framework for major companies and the way they are audited. For more, see: https://www.parliament.uk/site-information/glossary/white-paper/

127 Tavia Grant, "How One Company Levels the Pay Slope of Executives and Workers," *The Globe and Mail,* 16 November 2013. https://www.theglobeandmail.com/news/national/time-to-lead/how-one-company-levels-the-pay-slope-of-executives-and-workers/article15472738/.

128 Jim Ludema and Amber Johnson. "Gravity Payment's Dan Price on How He Measures Success after His $70k Experiment." Forbes, 28 August 2018. https://www.forbes.com/sites/amberjohnson-jimludema/2018/08/28/gravity-payments-dan-price-on-how-he-measures-success-after-his-70k-experiment/.

129 "Investors." www.lloydsbankinggroup.com. Accessed 27 June 2021. https://www.lloydsbankinggroup.com/globalassets/documents/investors/2017/2017feb22_lbg_summary_remuneration_announcement.pdf.

130 "Shareholders Meeting | Stock | Investor Relations | Samsung Global." Samsung Global. Accessed 27 June 2021. https://www.samsung.com/global/ir/governance-csr/general-meeting-of-shareholders/.

131 For more, see UK Policy White Paper ibid.

132 "Shared Prosperity: IFC and LS&Co. Team up to Reward Suppliers for Doing the Right Thing." Levi Strauss & Co, 5 November 2014. https://www.levistrauss.com/2014/11/05/shared-prosperity-ifc-and-levis-team-up-to-reward-suppliers-for-doing-the-right-thing/.

133 Number quoted for April 2020.

134 "Alpro (Alpro SCA) | Certified B Corporation." bcorporation. eu. Accessed 27 June 2021. https://bcorporation.eu/directory/alpro-alpro-sca.

135 "Engagement with Stakeholders – Sustainability – Yamaha Corporation," www.yamaha.com. Accessed 5 July 2021. https://www.yamaha.com/en/csr/stakeholder/.

136 "Consumer Debt." Investopedia. Accessed 27 June 2021.

https://www.investopedia.com/terms/c/consumer-debt.asp.

137 Anna Bradley and David Marjoribanks. "In Too Deep: an Investigation into Debt and Relationships." Relate, November 2017. Relate is a UK registered charity. https://www.relate.org.uk/sites/default/files/relate_problem_debt_report_web.pdf.

138 https://tech.newstatesman.com/security/data-breach-reports-ico.

139 "Annual Report 2016" Talk Talk Group. Accessed 27 June 2021. https://www.talktalkgroup.com/annualreports.

140 "The Ownership Dividend: The Economic Case for Employee Ownership," Employee Ownership (2018). https://employeeownership.co.uk/wp-content/uploads/The_Ownership_Dividend_The_economic_case_for_employee_ownership.pdf.

141 "Stakeholder Engagement." Nestle.com. Accessed 27 June 2021. https://www.nestle.com/csv/what-is-csv/stakeholder-engagement.

142 Mayra Rodriguez Valladares. "U.S. Corporates Continue to Gorge at the Debt Trough." Forbes, 10 April 2021. https://www.forbes.com/sites/mayrarodriguezvalladares/2021/04/10/us-corporates-continue-to-gorge-at-the-debt-trough/.

143 There may need to be some limited exceptions to the debt-to-equity ratio not exceeding 1:1, such as banks and property investment companies. Another way to target a sustainable level of debt is to keep the ratio between profit and interest at a high multiple – for example, planning for profit (after costs but before tax) to be at least four times the amount of interest payable on debt incurred by the company. This helps to give comfort as to cash flow security.

144 Attracta Mooney. "What a Gem." Campden FB, 31 July 2012. https://www.campdenfb.com/article/what-gem.

145 https://www.fool.com/investing/2020/05/31/heres-why-garmin-is-a-cash-flow-machine.aspx.

146 https://www.nytimes.com/2018/11/02/health/grocery-taxes-

oregon-washington-soda-tax.html.

[147] "When medical opinion in the United States came around to the view that the nation faced an epidemic of untreated pain, OxyContin sales representatives visited doctors across the United States, leaving them with gifts, free patient samples, and invitations to all-expenses-paid symposia — all actions that are known to impact prescribing. The widespread adoption of opioids for pain relief was further facilitated by marketing strategies that downplayed OxyContin's addictive potential and targeted primary care doctors, who continue to prescribe the majority of opioid pain relievers in many nations." This quote is from Tatyana Lyapustina and G. Caleb Alexander. "The Prescription Opioid Addiction and Abuse Epidemic: How It Happened and What We Can Do about It." *The Pharmaceutical Journal*, 11 June 015. https://pharmaceutical-journal.com/article/opinion/the-prescription-opioid-addiction-and-abuse-epidemic-how-it-happened-and-what-we-can-do-about-it.

[148] https://www.mottmac.com.

[149] "Sustainability." Aboutamazon.com. Accessed 27 June 2021. https://sustainability.aboutamazon.com/pdfBuilderDownload?name=goals&name=sustainable-operations&name=packaging-and-products&name=social-responsibility&name=employees-and-communities.

[150] Grace Gausden. "Amazon Launches 'Eco-Friendly' Platform to Reduce Amount of Packaging." This is Money, 29 October 2020. https://www.thisismoney.co.uk/money/bills/article-8888555/Amazon-launches-climate-friendly-platform-reduce-packaging.html.

[151] "Taxation and Our Total Economic Contribution to Public Finances 2018." Vodafone. Accessed 27 June 2021. https://www.vodafone.com/content/dam/vodcom/sustainability/pdfs/vodafone_2018_tax.pdf.

[152] "Microsoft by the Numbers." news.microsoft.com. Accessed 27 June 2021. https://news.microsoft.com/bythenumbers/en/water

[153] Jo Confino, "Unilever's Paul Polman: Challenging the Corporate Status Quo," *The Guardian*, 24 April 2012. https://www. theguardian.com/sustainable-business/paul-polman-unilever-sustainable-living-plan.

[154] For more, see: https://bcorporation.net.

[155] For more, see: https://www.goodbusinesscharter.com.

[156] "Why Was IR Developed? | Integrated Reporting," Integrated Reporting. Accessed 5 July 2021. https://integratedreporting.org/ why-the-need-for-change/why-was-developed/.

[157] The British Academy, "Principles for Purposeful Business | the British Academy." The British Academy, 2019. https://www. thebritishacademy.ac.uk/publications/future-of-the-corporation-principles-for-purposeful-business/.

[158] "Responsible Business." Saïd Business School. Accessed 27 June 2021. https://www.sbs.ox.ac.uk/research/centres-and-initiatives/ responsible-business.

[159] https://www.mars.com/news-and-stories/articles/economics-mutuality-foundation.

[160] "The Purposeful Company – Transform British Business." Accessed 27 June 2021. http://www.biginnovationcentre-purposeful-company.com/.

[161] Jason Mitchell. "How Corporate Governance Can Potentially Boost South Korean Shareholder Returns." Man Institue, June 2016. https://www.man.com/maninstitute/how-corporate-governance-can-potentially-boost-south-korean-shareholder-returns.

[162] Bryan Harris, "President Moon's tricky mission to tame Korea Inc", *Financial Times*, 12 September 2017. https://www.ft.com/ content/fa1e3e00-947b-11e7-bdfa-eda243196c2c.

[163] Byoung-Hoon Lee, "Labour unions and worker representation in South Korea", September 2019, pp.15 & 25. https://www.

researchgate.net/publication/335895191_Labour_unions_and_worker_representation_in_South_Korea.

[164] Felix I. Lessambo, "Corporate Governance in the United States of America." The International Corporate Governance System, 2014, 46–80. https://doi.org/10.1057/9781137360014_5.

[165] Holly J. Gregory, Rebecca Graspas, and Claire H Holland. "Corporate Governance and Directors' Duties in the United States: Overview." 1 May 2020. https://uk.practicallaw.thomsonreuters.com/w-011-8693.

[166] Holly J. Gregory, Rebecca Grapsas and Claire H. Holland, "Corporate Governance and Directors' Duties in the United States: Overview". See: https://uk.practicallaw.thomsonreuters.com/w-011-8693.

[167] Scott Dyreng, Bradley P. Lindsey, and Jacob R. Thornock. "Exploring the Role Delaware Plays as a Domestic Tax Haven." SSRN, 24 September 2012. https://doi.org/10.2139/ssrn.1737937.

[168] S.172 Companies Act 2006: https://www.legislation.gov.uk/ukpga/2006/46/section/172.

[169] The Companies (Miscellaneous Reporting) Regulations 2018: https://www.legislation.gov.uk/ukdsi/2018/9780111170298

[170] The UK Corporate Governance Code, Financial Reporting Council. 2018. https://www.frc.org.uk/getattachment/88bd8c45-50ea-4841-95b0-d2f4f48069a2/2018-UK-Corporate-Governance-Code-FINAL.PDF. The Wates Corporate Governance Principles for Large Private Companies contain similar language to the Code regarding the contribution of companies to wider society and the importance of engagement with stakeholders.

[171] Christoph H. Seibt and Sabrina Kulenkamp. "Corporate Governance and Directors' Duties in Germany: Overview." Accessed 7 July 2021. https://uk.practicallaw.thomsonreuters.com/8-502-1574.

[172] Gilbert Kreiger. "Handelsblatt Explains: Why German Corporate Governance Is so Different." Handelsblatt, 28 February 2018. https://www.handelsblatt.com/english/companies/handelsblatt-explains-why-german-corporate-governance-is-so-different/23581290.html.

[173] The Report on Corporate Governance for South Africa was published in November 2016. For more, see: https://www.pwc.co.za/en/publications/king4.html

[174] "Review of Corporate Governance Reporting." Financial Reporting Council. November 2020. https://www.frc.org.uk/getattachment/c22f7296-0839-420e-ae03-bdce3e157702/Governance-Report-2020-2611.pdf.

[175] The principle of "comply or explain" means that, if a company chooses to depart from the requirements of the corporate governance code, it must explain in its annual report to shareholders which parts of the code it has departed from and why.

[176] "Review of Corporate Governance Reporting." Financial Reporting Council. November 2020. https://www.frc.org.uk/getattachment/c22f7296-0839-420e-ae03-bdce3e157702/Governance-Report-2020-2611.pdf.

[177] "A Guide to Corporate Governance Practices in the European Union." World Bank Group, 2015. http://documents.worldbank.org/curated/en/750681468001781687/A-guide-to-Corporate-Governance-practices-in-the-European-Union

[178] In Japan, for example, the extent of the problem of "death by overwork" is indicated by the fact that the Japanese language has a specific word for it: karoshi. Fernando Duarte. "Which Country Works the Longest Hours?" BBC, 2018. https://www.bbc.com/worklife/article/20180504-which-country-works-the-longest-hours.

[179] In his review for the *Financial Times*, Robert Armstrong concedes that "at some point in the indefinite future, the social

good and financial interests must converge. There are no investment returns at all on a planet left uninhabitable by climate change. But that is not the time horizon individual investors operate over (they might have just 20 years between acquiring significant assets to invest and retiring). And it is far beyond any corporation's planning horizon … Over a realistic time horizon, a wicked or 'anti-ESG' portfolio perfectly well might offer the best available return." For more, see Robert Armstrong. "The Fallacy of ESG Investing." *Financial Times*, 23 October 2020. https://www.ft.com/content/9e3e1d8b-bf9f-4d8c-baee-0b25c3113319.

[180] "Hot Air." *The Economist*, 22 May 2021. https://www.economist.com/leaders/2021/05/22/sustainable-finance-is-rife-with-greenwash-time-for-more-disclosure.

[181] "A Senseless Subsidy." *The Economist*, 16 May 2015. https://www.economist.com/briefing/2015/05/16/a-senseless-subsidy.

[182] "A Senseless Subsidy." *The Economist*, 16 May 2015. https://www.economist.com/briefing/2015/05/16/a-senseless-subsidy.

[183] Ann Pettifor. *The Production of Money: How to Break the Power of Bankers*. London: Verso, 2018, p.73.

[184] The upswing of the corporate credit cycle sees a tightening of corporate bond spreads (for a given credit rating) and a decline in the covenants that bond investors and leveraged loan providers require for new or re-financings of higher-risk borrowers. These are "covenant-lite" deals and are tracked by ratings agencies and investment banks as an indicator of how loose or tight the corporate bond market is. For more information, see: https://www.whitecase.com/sites/default/files/2019-07/restructuring-next-wave-cov-lite-debt.pdf.

[185] Franco Modigliani and Merton H. Miller. "The Cost of Capital, Corporation Finance and the Theory of Investment." *The American Economic Review* 48, no. 3 (1958): 261–97. Accessed 28 June 2021. http://www.jstor.org/stable/1809766.

[186] Data in this table was kindly submitted by Keith Haddow.

[187] A radical proposal would be to re-introduce the "double" liability imposed on UK bank shareholders from the late-19th to early-20th centuries. This would mean that in the event of a bank insolvency, shareholders would be required to contribute the original share capital of the bank again to recapitalise the institution. This ensured that shareholders were strongly incentivised to monitor bank risk-taking.

[188] While physical stores were forced to close, online trade surged, particularly in the grocery sector. According to Digital Commerce 360 estimates, in 2020 consumers spent $861.12 billion online with US merchants in 2020, up 44.0 per cent year over year, the highest annual US e-commerce growth in at least two decades, and nearly triple the 15.1 per cent jump in 2019. Ali Fareeha. "US Ecommerce Sales Grow 15.0% in 2018." Digital Commerce 360, 29 January 2021. https://www.digitalcommerce360.com/article/us-ecommerce-sales/.

[189] "Digital Services Tax." UK Government. Accessed 27 June 2021. https://www.gov.uk/government/publications/introduction-of-the-digital-services-tax/digital-services-tax.

[190] Elke Asen. "What European OECD Countries Are Doing about Digital Services Taxes." Tax Foundation, 25 March 2021. https://taxfoundation.org/digital-tax-europe-2020/.

[191] Note, however, that strategic concerns over vulnerabilities of a nation's economy are starting to make a belated entrance to policy decisions. The EU Merger Regulation, US antitrust laws and competition rules in other countries would need to be considered in this context.

[192] Dominic Walsh. "Diageo Toasts Recovery by Restarting £4.5bn Buyback." *The Times,* 13 May 2021. https://www.thetimes.co.uk/article/diageo-toasts-recovery-by-restarting-4-5bn-buyback-v6ttbk72w.

[193] Lazonick, Sakinç, and Hopkins. "Why Stock Buybacks Are Dangerous for the Economy." *Harvard Business Review,* 7 January 2020. https://hbr.org/2020/01/why-stock-buybacks-are-dangerous-for-the-economy.

[194] Leonore Palladino. "Examining Corporate Priorities: The Impact of Stock Buybacks on Workers, Communities and Investors." The Harvard Law School Forum on Corporate Governance, October 22, 2019. https://corpgov.law.harvard. edu/2019/10/22/examining-corporate-priorities-the-impact-of-stock-buybacks-on-workers-communities-and-investors/.

[195] Useem, Jerry. "Why Are Stock Buybacks so Popular?" The Atlantic, August 2019. https://www.theatlantic.com/magazine/ archive/2019/08/the-stock-buyback-swindle/592774/.

[196] Lazonick, Sakinç, and Hopkins. "Why Stock Buybacks Are Dangerous for the Economy." Harvard Business Review, 7 January 2020. https://hbr.org/2020/01/why-stock-buybacks-are-dangerous-for-the-economy.

[197] In the US in 2016 and 2017, according to JPMorgan Chase, up to 30 per cent of buybacks were being funded by issuing corporate bonds, thus creating debt obligations. For more, see: Gregory Calderone. "Bloomberg – Are You a Robot?" Bloomberg, 27 January 2019. https://www.bloomberg.com/news/ articles/2019-01-27/debt-financed-share-buybacks-dwindle-to-lowest-level-since-2009.

[198] www.businessinsider.com/larry-fink-letter-to-ceos-2015-4?IR=T

[199] On 16 March 2021, the CIA outlined what it said were "influence operations" pushed by Russia as well as Iran. It said Russian-linked individuals had spread unsubstantiated claims about President Biden ahead of the 3 November 2020 presidential election. It also said a disinformation campaign sought to undermine confidence in the broader election process. For more, see: "Russia's Putin Authorised Pro-Trump 'Influence' Campaign, US Intelligence Says." BBC, 17 March 2021. https://www.bbc. co.uk/news/world-us-canada-56423536.

[200] In Luxembourg, where each Member of Parliament represents 8,484 voters, it is possible to believe that a citizen could get one-on-one time to obtain assistance or make his or her views known.

In the UK, an MP serves, on average, 68,000 voters; in India, 1.5 million.

[201] Maggie Baska. "Work-Life Balance Is Getting More out of Kilter, Says CIPD Survey." People Management, 12 June 2019. https://www.peoplemanagement.co.uk/news/articles/work-life-balance-more-out-of-kilter-says-cipd-survey.

[202] In May 2018 a CIPD Wellbeing at Work survey suggested more than a fifth of organisations cited mental illness as the primary cause of long-term absence. For more, see "Health and Well-Being at Work." CIPD, 27 April 2021. https://www.cipd.co.uk/knowledge/culture/well-being/health-well-being-work

[203] Roger Boyes. "China's Pension Crisis Threatens Xi's Regime." The Times, 4 May 2021. https://www.thetimes.co.uk/article/its-chinas-pensioners-xi-jinping-should-fear-dtxvg0dv0.

[204] "China Allows Three Children in Major Policy Shift." BBC News, 31 May 2021. https://www.bbc.co.uk/news/world-asia-china-57303592.

[205] Ed Conway. "It's Time We Thought More about Procreation." The Times, 15 January 2021, sec. comment. https://www.thetimes.co.uk/article/it-s-time-we-thought-more-about-procreation-p0gnjhs5s.

[206] Lucy Kitson, and Travers Merrill. "The End of Coal Mining in South Wales: Lessons Learned from Industrial Transformation." International Institute for Sustainable Development, 18 May 2017, pp.1, 9. https://www.iisd.org/publications/end-coal-mining-south-wales-lessons-learned-industrial-transformation.

[207] Kitson and Merrill. Ibid, p.iii.

[208] "68% of the World Population Projected to Live in Urban Areas by 2050, Says UN." United Nations, 16 May 2018. https://www.un.org/development/desa/en/news/population/2018-revision-of-world-urbanization-prospects.html.
Note that urban expansion is complex. However, "Very often, urbanization is primarily the result of migration. This is shown

by the fact that fertility rates in urban areas tend to be lower than those of rural areas." (World Migration Report 2015, p.19).

[209] "62 Percent of Workers Would Relocate for a Job, Survey Finds." rh-us.mediaroom.com. Accessed 27 June 2021. http://rh-us.mediaroom.com/2019-01-15-62-Percent-Of-Workers-Would-Relocate-For-A-Job-Survey-Finds.

[210] In low-income countries, rural-urban migration tends to leave large numbers of disconnected young males in cities, with rural communities disproportionately made up of women, young children, and the elderly. While there is some evidence that rural communities can benefit – for example, by labour shortages exerting upward pressure on wages – it is more likely that women will bear the economic and social burden, while rates of child labour may increase. Remittances sent by family members working in cities or abroad are important financial lifelines, but cannot fully compensate for the loss of human capital that would otherwise have provided local family and community support and contributions to healthcare and education.

[211] Nathalie Bélorgey et al, 'Social Impact of Emigration and Rural-Urban Migration in Central and Eastern Europe (VT/2010/001),' Gesellschaft für Versicherungswissenschaft und –gestaltung, Köln, Germany, 2012.

[212] "Learning the Hard Way." *The Economist*, 2 January 2016. https://www.economist.com/europe/2016/01/02/learning-the-hard-way.

[213] "Equipping citizens with the knowledge and skills necessary to achieve their full potential, to contribute to an increasingly interconnected world, and to convert better skills into better lives needs to become a more central preoccupation of policy makers around the world." This quote is from Andreas Schleicher. "PISA 2018 Insights and Interpretations." OECD, 2019. https://www.oecd.org/pisa/PISA.

[214] In 2015, the European Court of Human Rights disposed of some 45,576 applications, suggesting that individual rights

often come into conflict. As a possible way forward see also "Relational Rights: A world-inclusive and relationships-affirming understanding of the rights of every human person"; Emily Ho, Matthew Ferguson, Jeremy Ive and Michael Schluter, published by Relational Research, 2021, (available from: www.relationalresearch.org).

[215] Note that the problem here was exacerbated by the use of a referendum – an instrument which can create a policy without a government committed to enact it.

[216] "Litigation Funding to Double in 5 Years." Lawyer Monthly | Legal News Magazine, 25 May 2019. https://www.lawyer-monthly.com/2019/03/litigation-funding-to-double-in-5-years/.

[217] Louisa Clarence-Smith. "Funder Backs Claim against KPMG over Carillion." *The Times*, 20 May 2021. https://www.thetimes.co.uk/article/funder-backs-claim-against-kpmg-over-carillion-kns2l0twt.

[218] Janna Anderson and Lee Rainie, "The Future of Truth and Misinformation Online", Pew Research Center, 19 October 2017. See: https://www.pewresearch.org/internet/2017/10/19/the-future-of-truth-and-misinformation-online/.

[219] According to a member of the US Senate Homeland Security Committee, following quarterback Colin Kaepernick's decision to kneel during the playing of the American national anthem, Russian internet trolls took both sides of the social media debate – #TakeAKnee and #BoycottNFL. Pierre Thomas and Jack Date, "Russian internet trolls pushing #TakeAKnee, #BoycottNFL to sow discord in US: Senator", ABC News, 27 September 2017. https://abcnews.go.com/Politics/russian-internet-trolls-calling-takeaknee-boycottnf-sow-discord.

[220] Janna Anderson and Lee Rainie, "The Future of Truth and Misinformation Online", Pew Research Center, 19 October 2017. See: https://www.pewresearch.org/internet/2017/10/19/the-future-of-truth-and-misinformation-online/.

221 https://eur-lex.europa.eu/legal-content/EN/
TXT/?uri=LEGISSUM%3Aai0017.

222 "The principle of subsidiarity". https://eur-lex.europa.eu/legal-content/EN/TXT/HTML/?uri=LEGISSUM:ai0017.

223 "Brexit Day: The Story of the UK Leaving the EU in Key Quotes." BBC News, 31 January 2020. https://www.bbc.co.uk/news/uk-46920529.

224 Owen Dyer. "Covid-19: Many Poor Countries Will See Almost No Vaccine next Year, Aid Groups Warn." *BMJ* no. 371, 11 December 2020). https://doi.org/10.1136/bmj.m4809.

225 Michelle Nichols and Stephanie Nebehay, "Global Officials Urge Rich Countries to Donate Excess COVID-19 Vaccines, Money to Help End Pandemic," Reuters, 15 April 2021. https://www.reuters.com/business/healthcare-pharmaceuticals/global-officials-urge-rich-countries-donate-excess-covid-19-vaccines-money-help-2021-04-15/.

226 Moira Fagan and Christine Huang, "A Look at How People around the World View Climate Change," Pew Research Center, 18 April 2019. https://www.pewresearch.org/fact-tank/2019/04/18/a-look-at-how-people-around-the-world-view-climate-change/.

227 Dan M. Kahan. "What Is the 'Science of Science Communication'?" papers.ssrn.com. Rochester, NY, 10 February 2015. https://papers.ssrn.com/sol3/papers.cfm?abstract_id=2562025.

228 Moira Fagan and Christine Huang, "A Look at How People around the World View Climate Change," Pew Research Center, 18 April 2019. https://www.pewresearch.org/fact-tank/2019/04/18/a-look-at-how-people-around-the-world-view-climate-change/.

229 Dan M. Kahan. "What Is the 'Science of Science Communication'?" papers.ssrn.com. Rochester, NY, February

10, 2015. https://papers.ssrn.com/sol3/papers.cfm?abstract_id=2562025.

[230] Kylie Gordon, "A Bridge amidst Disaster: Stanford Researchers Find California Wildfires Shrink Partisan Differences about Climate Change Strategies," Stanford News, 25 September 2020. https://news.stanford.edu/2020/09/25/california-wildfires-shrink-partisan-differences-climate-change/.

[231] Andrew Revkin, "Most Americans Now Worry about Climate Change—and Want to Fix It," *National Geographic*, 23 January 2019. https://www.nationalgeographic.com/environment/article/climate-change-awareness-polls-show-rising-concern-for-global-warming.

[232] "Never Waste a Crisis: Companies Invest to 'Recover Better' from COVID-19", United Nations, 24 June 2020. https://www.un.org/en/coronavirus/never-waste-crisis-corporations-invest-'recover-better'-covid-19.

[233] Note that in 2018, across 27 nations surveyed by Pew Research Center, people were more dissatisfied than satisfied with the way democracy is working in their country. In Mexico, Greece, Brazil and Spain, dissatisfaction ran at over 80 per cent. For more, see: Richard Wike, Laura Silver, and Alexandra Castillo. "Many People around the World Are Unhappy with How Democracy Is Working." Pew Research Center, 29 April 2019. https://www.pewresearch.org/global/2019/04/29/many-across-the-globe-are-dissatisfied-with-how-democracy-is-working/.

[234] Charles Handy, "What is a business for?" *Harvard Business Review*, December 2002. https://hbr.org/2002/12/whats-a-business-for.

[235] Relational Analytics. Accessed 27 June 2021. https://www.relational-analytics.com.

A WORD ON RELATIONAL RESEARCH

Over centuries, there has been much research, study, and reflection on individual relationships as well as on organisational relationships – from different and indeed contrasting philosophical, psychological, sociological, historical, economic, financial, and political orientations.

Further, some of all that has emerged from and focused on the intellectual and academic level, while some has sought to illuminate and improve policy and practice.

Relational Research seeks to contribute to all the current conversations about 'Relational Thinking', its meaning within the Christian and Jewish faith traditions, and its application to the organisation and conduct of healthy human relationships in public and private life. The aim is that the results of such research may bring public benefit.

This book has had a long gestation period – over 15 years. We welcome thoughtful comments and reflections from practitioners in both the private and public sector at the level both of principle and of practice.

Please visit our website: www.relationalresearch.org